1247

PRESERVATION
PIONEER

1247

PRESERVATION PIONEER

The story of Britain's first privately
preserved standard gauge steam
locomotive

Capt W. G. (Bill) Smith
V.R.D., C.Eng, F.I.Marine E., R.N.R.

Silver Link Publishing Ltd

First published in 1991

British Library Cataloguing in Publication Data
Smith, W. G. (William G.)
1247: preservation pioneer: the story of Britain's first privately preserved
standard gauge steam locomotive.
1. Great Britain.   Steam locomotives
I. Title
625.2610941

ISBN 0 947971 57 2

Silver Link Publishing Ltd
The Trundle
Ringstead Road
Great Addington
Kettering
Northamptonshire NN14 4BW

Typeset byThe Typefoundry Limited, Northampton
Printed in Great Britain by Woolnough Bookbinding Ltd, Irthlingborough, Northants
and bound by Mackays of Chatham PLC, Chatham, Kent.

Cover photographs
Front: 1247 approaching Darnholm on the North Yorks
Moors Railway, July 1976. (J. Winkley)

Back: Top left: as No 68446, Shed Pilot
at King's Cross Top Shed, April 1959 (P. N. Townend);
Top right: restored to GNR livery as No 1247 at Marshmoor, July
1959 (H. C. Smith); Above left: at work on the Keighley & Worth
Valley Railway in June 1966 (W. Hubert Foster);
Above right: Bill Smith handing the locomotive over at the
National Railway Museum, December 1980
(Yorkshire Evening Press).

CONTENTS

To those 'wonderful railway friends';
my family, for their patience
and understanding; and my father,
for sowing the seed so well.

FOREWORD

by
Capt Peter Manisty MBE, RN (Ret'd)
Vice President, Association of Railway Preservation Societies

1990 was Railway Preservation Year, marking 30 years of railway preservation and highlighting the three pioneer volunteer preserved railways – the narrow gauge Talyllyn, and the standard gauge Bluebell and Middleton railways. The story has now been rounded off by this epic book, and I am honoured and delighted to provide this Foreword.

This is the tale of what a one-man-band achieved during those 30 years. Bill Smith's No 1247 provided a solo performance throughout – not only was she the first privately owned steam locomotive to operate on British Rail (beating *Flying Scotsman* by a short head), but her career has spanned the three decades of railway preservation, from the hauling of the 'Blue Belle' from London Bridge to Sheffield Park and back on 1 April 1962, with Dr Beeching on board, to the hauling of the 'Middleton Pioneer' on that railway at Leeds on 23 June 1990. She is now steaming for posterity as part of the National Railway Museum's collection (to whom Bill Smith donated the locomotive in 1980), and is appearing as an honoured guest at RailFair 91 in Sacramento, California, in May 1991.

This splendid book unfolds the incredible story – so far – of Bill Smith's locomotive, whose achievements richly merit the hoisting of the Royal Naval signal: 'Manoeuvres well executed'!

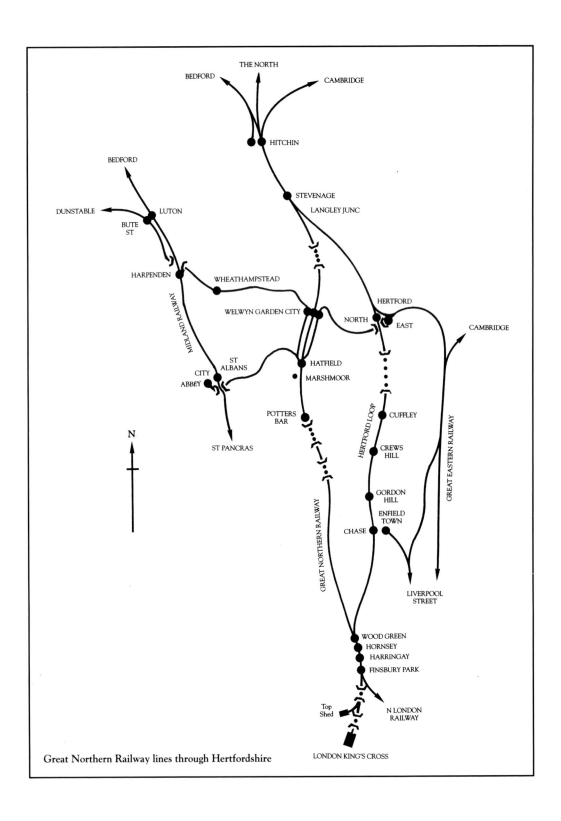

THE NORTH

BEDFORD

CAMBRIDGE

HITCHIN

STEVENAGE
LANGLEY JUNC

BEDFORD

DUNSTABLE

LUTON

BUTE
ST

HARPENDEN

WHEATHAMPSTEAD

MIDLAND RAILWAY

WELWYN GARDEN CITY

HERTFORD

NORTH

EAST

CAMBRIDGE

ST
ALBANS

CITY

ABBEY

HATFIELD

MARSHMOOR

GREAT EASTERN RAILWAY

N

ST PANCRAS

POTTERS
BAR

HERTFORD LOOP

CUFFLEY

CREWS
HILL

GORDON
HILL

GREAT NORTHERN RAILWAY

ENFIELD
TOWN

CHASE

LIVERPOOL
STREET

WOOD GREEN
HORNSEY
HARRINGAY
FINSBURY PARK

Top
Shed

N LONDON
RAILWAY

LONDON KING'S CROSS

Great Northern Railway lines through Hertfordshire

INTRODUCTION

The life of a railway servant at the turn of the century was hard and poorly paid, yet in all grades the level of dedication to the job and loyalty toward 'the Company' was refreshingly high. No doubt the security of the job, with its prospects for regular life-long employment, provided the incentive.

When my father left school at the age of 15, he secured employment with the Great Northern Railway as a telegraph lad in Newark South signal box. My awareness of his railway service did not commence until I was about five years of age, by which time he was signalman at Harringay Up Goods, and the family home was at Gordon Hill on the Hertford North branch.

Harringay Up Goods box was a tall gaunt structure controlling the south ends of the Ferme Park Goods complex, its adjoining Hornsey Loco, and the flyover access to Hornsey Down Side Yard. The 'movements' at that time were numerous enough to provide interest for a keen young railway-man, but it was apparent to me that the adjoining busy main and suburban lines in his full view, but outside his control, would soon lure him to better things.

In those years, Enfield was a convenient and popular dormitory for railmen in the King's Cross and Liverpool Street areas, and I regularly contrived to travel with my father when he was coming off duty. Trains close to the shift-change times would carry more than their fair share of railmen, and it was customary for footplate and other grades to congregate in their 'exclusive' compart-ments. Understandably, the workings and incidents of the day took pride of place in the conversation, only to be interrupted if a current Test Match had reached the 'nail-biting' stage. Sharing one of those journeys with him, I was in my element, enjoying a worm's-eye view of what to me was already the most wonderful element in my world – the Great Northern Railway.

Family excursions were few in those days compared with the freedom we enjoy today. Such as were possible within a restricted family budget were aided by those treasured facilities, the free 'family' pass and 'privilege' tickets, the former being carefully preserved for the family holidays. The necessity to travel by rail was always a delight for me, but must have been something of a busman's holiday for father, who bore it all good-naturedly. Those wonderful railway holidays took us throughout the length and breadth of the country, and it is true to say that I learned more geography thereby than in any classroom.

When travelling with father, I always endeavoured to manoeuvre him to the point on the platform where the locomotive would come to rest. On one such day, the train engine was Gresley GNR 0-6-2 'N2' Class No 1752 allocated to Hornsey MPD and in the charge of Driver Bill Rocket. What a wonderful name for a driver! A large man with a ruddy, round smiling face and 'handlebar' moustache, he recognised father and invited us to travel with him on the footplate. My excitement was unbounded, and from Gordon Hill to Finsbury Park I stood in the 'well' with its excellent view of the firebox but little else!

That trip was to prove the first of several on the footplate of No 1752 with Bill Rocket, and I progressed to more comfortable and instructive accommodation. Those were the years in which locomen were personally allocated to an9 engine which they 'shared' with another pair of men. The standard of locomotive care was in consequence high, and it was no uncommon sight to see enginemen cleaning down and oiling round after having run round their train at Gordon Hill, Cuffley or Hertford North. The pride of these men in their Ivatt 'N1s' and Gresley 'N2s' was no less than that of their counterparts entrusted with more glamorous engines on the main line.

Maintenance of the tight North London Suburban diagrams called for a high level of skill and concentration by those drivers in good weather conditions, but stories of their

performance in winter weather with nil visibility in 'pea soup' fog and without the train control aids we know today, are legend. Road knowledge was as much a matter for ears as for eyes. Overbridges, underbridges, lineside walls and fences, points and crossovers, were all vital ingredients in an exciting cacophony of sound, and built up in the mind of the driver and fireman alike a detailed and accurate picture of the exact yard by yard location of their train.

In those days, the Hertford North branch was full of interest and traffic was not confined, as some might expect, to GN suburban trains connecting Hertford North with King's Cross and Moorgate. At that time the North London Railway (later to be absorbed into the LMS) had 'running powers' out of Broad Street extending to Gordon Hill, and their low-roofed 'birdcage' sets comprised 10 or 12 four-wheeled cars worked by North London Railway 4-4-0 tanks.

So much for the bread-and-butter suburban stuff. It was leavened with all the

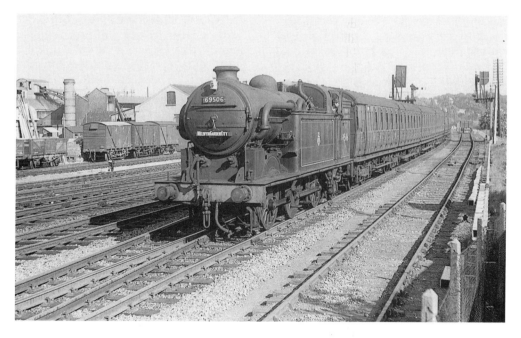

A Gresley 'N2' 0-6-2T in BR days: No 69506 arriving at New Southgate with a Welwyn Garden City service. (*P. N. Townend*)

'spice' and excitement of 'fitted' goods and fish trains, and long, loose-coupled coal trains and 'empties' diverted to relieve the main-line 'bottle-necks'. Mixed 'unfitted' goods trains and empty coaching stock to Enfield Chase Yard made up the daily round of never-ending excitement.

In the early 1920s, father was transferred to King's Cross (East) box and later, upon its commissioning, as regulator in what became known as the 'new power box' at King's Cross, which absorbed the functions of both the East and West boxes which were then demolished. The considerably better level of his income brought about the removal of the family home to a pleasant new house at Enfield Chase where, through a conveniently spaced row of poplars, my bedroom window commanded an excellent view of the line, some 200 yards away.

I was quickly able to identify the various locomotive types by their beat and work pattern on the changing gradients there-abouts. I would lie awake late into the night listening for the first sound of each approaching train. An up coal train would come within ear-shot midway between Crews Hill and Gordon Hill some miles away, as its Gresley Class '02' beat fussily up the gradient. This changed, as the train approached Gordon Hill, to a clanking as the regulator was closed and brake applied for the falling gradient through to Enfield Chase and Grange Park. These trains, after bedtime, always called for a 'peep' as they passed, the van, with its shrill screaming brakes and sparks flying from its wheels, striving, with the locomotive, to keep 60 impatient and loaded wagons in check.

Instances occurred where the guard, having 'dropped off', failed to 'stretch' the train with his brake, leaving it all to the locomotive. With the sharply varying grades, the loose couplings could become suddenly strained when the regulator was re-opened to climb the sharp rise between Grange Park and Winchmore Hill, and trains occasionally became 'divided'. With such happenings well in mind, the necessity to 'observe' the guards' vigilance was of importance to this already highly involved enthusiast.

It is interesting to note that these Gresley Class '02' 2-8-0 locomotives, with their tractive effort of 36,470 lb, enabled 80-wagon coal trains to be worked between Peterborough and London, but the load was restricted to 60 wagons when working up via the Hertford North loop because of the numerous short, sharp and varied gradients between Cuffley and Wood Green, at which point the main line was rejoined.

From about ten years of age, it became customary for me to spend a large part of the school holidays with my paternal grand-parents in Newark, travelling by train from King's Cross. My favourite train was the four o'clock to Leeds, which departed from Platform 10 and which later became the 'West Riding'.

I was placed in the care of the guard at King's Cross, and his brake was second only to the footplate of one of those superb and lively Ivatt 'Atlantics' which worked the diagram at that time. My companions ranged from dogs and cats to pigeons and poultry, together with boxes and parcels of all sizes and shapes. The guard's brakes of that time were, however, ideal for human passengers with their convenient 'ducket' windows which provided a clear view along the side of the train, both forward to the engine and to the rear.

The sharp working of the locomotives on that diagram, replaced as I grew older by Gresley 'A3' 'Pacifics', was always a delight to me, as was that of my up favourite, the 10.23 ex-Newark, due King's Cross at 13.03. Present-day journeys by '125' on the East Coast Main Line, with their sharp accelera-tion and drastically reduced journey times, can never eradicate from my mind the splendid time-keeping accomplished with heavy loads by steam enginemen on that route prior to dieselisation.

Arrival of the train at Newark involved transfer to another mode of travel – the station horse-bus. This rather splendid contraption was arranged for the accom-modation of some 12 or so passengers inside, with baggage aloft. With wooden, steel-shod

Gresley '02' Class 2-8-0 No 63940 leaving Grantham on a short train for the Highdyke branch in the early 1960s. (P. N. *Townend*)

wheels, it rumbled noisily over the cobbled streets, delivering its passengers in turn throughout the town – only the well-turned-out horse seemed oblivious of the clatter!

After the shortest possible time to convey personal family messages and news to my grandparents, I would ask to be allowed out for a quick visit to Barnby signal box, to which I was able to run in about 15 minutes. Barnby was on the main line between Newark South and Balderton, and the object of my urgent reconnoitre was to ascertain the current shift of Signalman Bob Dawson, a contemporary of my father. Once I had located Bob, I could plan the whole of my holiday, carefully ensuring that I kept clear of the cabin whenever there was any sign of his opposite number. He was by name Walter Field, a strict disciplinarian, and to have appeared in his presence would have

been to invite a fate worse than death!

When Bob was on early turn, my aim was to be clear of my grandmother's Scots authority by 8 am, armed, she insisted, with carefully prepared sandwiches to sustain a growing boy but, in fact, frequently sufficient to maintain a platoon of infantry. The 8 am departure was firmly dependent upon conditions which were inflexible at all times. A thorough grooming extending well behind and below the ears, a slowly eaten breakfast and last, but not least, shoes polished bright – all over! Upon this last point, the lady could be a tartar!

'Remember Willie!' she would intone, 'you may one day find yourself with little money, wearing worn clothes which have seen better days, and old shoes. But, if the shoes are well polished, you will always look worth an extra shilling!'

Bless her heart. I was many times to recall her and those guide-lines when applying a critical eye to men during my time in the Service – but that comes much later.

Whilst tolerating a daily disappearance 'to the railway' on weekdays, it was, with my grandmother, a case of 'never on Sundays'. On those days, morning and evening, I accompanied my grandparents, aunts, uncles, and cousins in strict order of family seniority to London Road Church. It would be both un-Christian and untrue were I not to admit that during many a sermon my mind would stray to Barnby box, particularly if the distracting whistle of a non-stop caught my ears as it hurried through Newark station. I am quite sure that the dear lady froze at the sound, as she pictured it luring me to the devil, so I did all I could to put her mind at rest by singing extra lustily through the next hymn.

To get back to the box. In those days it was a squat cabin with a pitched slate roof, situated to the south of the road crossing gates on the down side of the track. Beautifully cosy in winter and with generous sliding windows for summer use, it housed a 15-lever frame to control both up and down lines, a crossover and road and pedestrian gate locks.

In those early days, I was not tall enough either to reach the block instruments or operate the levers, but Bob took me through each movement with great patience. What a wonderful vantage point it was too! Sufficiently close to the up road to smell the steam and oil, whilst the down, with its falling gradient to the curve into Newark station, gave the impression that the train would hurtle clean through the box.

It was customary to 'hold' up to four or five coal and mixed 'unfitted' goods trains in the up accommodation sidings controlled by Newark South. Every opportunity between passenger and/or class 'A' goods trains had to be taken to work one of the goods forward. A goods train so released had to reach Claypole or Hougham to the south before it could again take 'refuge' and avoid delaying following fast traffic. The goods were in the

main worked by 'asthmatic' Ivatt 0-6-0 Class 'J6' locomotives which, when released to us from Newark South, worked their way slowly and laboriously up the bank. What a relief it was to give 'out of section' to Newark South and pray that he would not quickly push something else at us before we had been able to re-settle our nerves. It really was a nail-biting experience, willing the locomotive up the long straight bank whilst visualising train upon train grinding to a halt because our line to the south was 'blocked'. I could visualise a Fat Controller and Station Master descending simultaneously upon Barnby cabin and venting their wrath upon both of us. Occasionally one of those 'unfitted' goods would be hauled by a Robinson 2-8-0 Class 'O1' which, with its greater power and smaller driving wheels, got its train moving more easily and 'cleared' more quickly and comfortably – for us all!

At last came the day when I could reach the block instruments and pull off the 'boards' – with the exception of that stubborn up distant (with its assisting foot-rest). My excitement and pride knew no bounds! From that point Bob acted as telegraph-lad and kept the Train Register, allowing me, under his eagle eye, to 'work' the box.

Barnby box, as I knew it, has disappeared. The present box is a grand affair and gives the impression of being a 'power box', controlling 'everything that moves' between Peterborough and Doncaster! It is sighted north of the road crossing on the up side. With incorporation of colour light signalling, it will have been possible to dispense with that horrible foot-rest for pulling off the 'Up Distant'.

The Hertford North branch as we know it today leaves the main line at Wood Green, but originally terminated at Enfield Chase with an 'island' platform layout, facilities for running-round and generous support sidings.

When the branch was extended to Hertford North, a new station was built some 200 yards down Windmill Hill, to the east. The line was extended to Cuffley in 1910 and to Hertford North in 1918. Originally only a single track beyond Cuffley, it was later doubled and extended to rejoin the main line at Langley Junction, just south of Stevenage.

This 'Hertford loop' was to prove invaluable as a bypass of the Greenwood–Potters Bar and Welwyn North bottle-necks on the East Coast Main Line, and became used not only in emergencies and at times of main-line PW 'possession', but also as an alternative route by which some two dozen trains each day were diagrammed, interspersed among the busy suburban pattern.

The old Enfield Chase station and yard was adapted after 1910 to serve as a Goods Distribution Depot, for which purpose it was ideal. The platform area was used to construct a refrigerated warehouse-type structure for Fyffes Bananas, whilst in the yard, areas were adapted to house stoneware goods for Turner & Newall and to provide storage pounds for large quantities of coal for the Co-operative Society, Tyne Main Coal Co, and Herbert Clarke. The more remote sidings between the old and new stations were used to stable main-line stock, normally worked in and out by Ivatt Class 'N1' or Gresley 'N2' locomotives.

To support the goods yard activities, three booked goods trains were involved on each weekday, the daily flow of wagons averaging a hundred or so both in and out. The locomotives diagrammed for these trains were customarily Ivatt Class 'J6' or 'N1', or Gresley 'N2', and having brought in a train, they were then employed marshalling the yard before departing later in the day with a string of empties.

This meant that, under normal conditions, two locomotives were busily shunting at most times of the day, whilst on Saturdays at least one would be present maintaining service to the railhead distributors.

At the busy road entrance to this hive of railway activity stood a brick-built, single-storey office for weighbridge and other clerks whose prime duty in life appeared to be the suppression of railway 'involvement' by small boys! This was the reason, although the yard was no more than half-a-mile from home, that I always went by cycle. Approaching the gate I would dismount and walk purposefully forward into the yard, wheeling the cycle on my right hand so that it hid my short trousers from the gaze of the eagle-eyed clerks. Rarely was I turned away, and so was able to spend many happy Saturdays and holidays there.

My favourite vantage point was close to where the locomotives came to rest after drawing forward between each shunt. A wave and a smile did not always work, but on many occasions it did, and I would drop the cycle and run to accept the offered footplate ride. I quickly came to recognise the drivers who were 'co-operative', and if one such could be 'contacted' at the beginning of the week, prospects were good for a full 'footplate' week.

The conditions were ideal for initiation into footplate practice; it was all done at a pretty leisurely pace with constant change of direction from forward to reverse and vice versa. The climate was therefore ideal for putting questions to a crew who were not under pressure and to whom questions, carefully timed, could not prove a distraction. There is no doubt that the kindness and patience of the men who worked that yard from about 1926 to 1929 brought about my rapid and distinct change of interest from S&T to motive power. From that point, it became my firm resolve to become an engine driver!

As I recollect, it was at about this time that I made my first railway blunder. My father decided that the time had come to discuss with me the question of a career. To me the future was quite clear – with the excellent railway 'schooling' I had received, my mind was made up and it is not surprising that I was able to announce my decision, with pride and alacrity. It took far less time for him to tell me in no uncertain terms that if I took one step toward the railway, he would 'cut me off without a shilling'!

It was respect for him, rather than the thought of losing what must have been a rather nebulous inheritance, which kept me clear of the railway, and instead I took up employment with the Anglo-Persian Oil Co in London. This did have one bonus – it involved daily travel by train to the City, not to mention the requirement for five years of intensive study of Mechanical Engineering in the evenings at the Northampton Polytechnic in St John Street, Clerkenwell (now the City of London University).

In the late 1930s, it became increasingly obvious that the occupation of many young men would shortly undergo a dramatic change. At the time I was Assistant to Eric Truscott, the Chief Inspecting Engineer of the Oil Co, a retired Lieutenant Commander (E) Royal Navy. In the course of conversation he reminded me that in my current employment I would be classified 'reserved', were the balloon to go up! His advice was 'join the Navy as quickly as you can'.

A visit to the Admiralty threatened to bring about an emergency meeting of the Board! I was very firmly informed that the Navy had no requirement for Engineer Officers and were quite unaware of any impending emergency which could change that situation! Obviously all was well in their world!

Further consultation with Eric Truscott resulted in my visiting the Royal Naval Recruiting Office in Edgware. I was greeted somewhat brusquely by a long-retired, but still very 'prickly', Chief Gunners Mate. Stating politely that I wished to join the Royal Navy, he quickly retorted, 'We ain't got no vacancies 'cept for Cooks an' Stewards'. I then proceeded to explain to him that I was useless even at boiling water, and as for stewarding, I was unable to pour a cup of tea without scalding my foot.

This, I sensed, increased his 'prickle factor', but he reached for a clip-board to which were attached a number of very official-looking sheets.

'Ow abart internal combustion injins?' he barked.

I quickly replied, 'Oh yes, sir, you mean petrol and diesel engines.'

'Don't call me sir, call me Chief,' he spat, 'and don't get fresh with me. The Admirality in this 'ere sheet ses quite plain, internal combustion injins, and if they ses internal combustion injins, they means internal combustion injins, not your petrol and diesel injins.'

'Quite so, Chief,' I replied meekly, 'but with respect, petrol and diesel engines are internal combustion engines.'

To my surprise he did not go through the roof, but instead reached for a form which, with my answers to his questions, he proceeded laboriously to complete. I gained the impression that the form to be completed for a Cook or Steward entry would have been both simpler and shorter.

'I shall send this 'ere through to the Admirality,' he threatened, 'and let them sort out you and yer diesel and petrol injins. It clearly ses 'ere as I told yer, internal combustion injins.'

Obviously Their Lordships' understanding of internal combustion engines coincided with mine, since four weeks later I was commanded to report to RN Barracks, Chatham, 'for trade-test and MTBs for disposal'. Whether I or the MTBs were 'for disposal' was at the time unclear to me, but, as the massive prison-like gates at Chatham clanged shut behind me, the expression 'Meredith, you're in' came forcibly to mind.

My stay in the Barracks was short-lived, and after a week in the Dockyard converting two pieces of steel into the renowned Naval 'Strap and Block' with the aid of hammer, chisel and file only, the 'disposal' question was clarified for me – I was drafted to the 11th MTB Flotilla based at Dover.

Some 16 months later (included in which were seven months stay in RN Hospital Chatham), information of some kind must have filtered through to Admiralty of a requirement for Engineer Officers, for a signal was made to Dover announcing that I was promoted to Sub Lieut (E) and instructing me to report to RN Barracks Portsmouth on the following Monday morning, suitably kitted out for a two-week Officers Divisional Course.

The Course comprised some 60 or so officers, predominantly two-stripe 'direct entry' Surgeons and 'Fang Farriers', but with a few lower-deck 'promotions' like myself. The officer in charge of the Course was a Lieutenant Commander Goodyer RN and to my horror he called out my name before any proceedings took place. I had immediate visions of some previously undetected crime having caught up with me to blight my Naval career. Or could it be that an earlier meritorious act of gallantry had brought some high award – to be presented by the Commander in Chief, no less?

I was not kept long in suspense. The Course Officer said, 'You've just come from an MTB Flotilla, Smith,' to which I spluttered, 'Yes, sir'.

'Well, there's no Divisional Course for you,' he pressed on. 'The Engineer Officer of the 1st MGB Flotilla got himself shot last night and you've got his job.'

And so that 'pier-head jump' sent me straight to Lowestoft to take up my first appointment as Engineer Officer responsible for all that went in and out, up and down, and round and round in a Flotilla of eight MGBs.

To avoid the reader becoming confused, it should be explained that these Naval references merely serve to bridge the gap in my railway exploits from the late 1930s to the late 1950s, during which period I was 'otherwise engaged'.

My railway interest was not, however, dead – merely dormant, awaiting a suitable opportunity to re-emerge. Such an opportunity arose almost 20 years later, in 1957, when a Naval colleague Tim Bolland told me that he had joined British Railways as a

premium apprentice. I revealed my railway interest – and expressed envy at his job.

Tim was posted to Southern Region and was the most fortunate of young men in being appointed to work under Sidney W. Smart CBE, the Chief Operating Superintendent. Through Tim Bolland I was privileged to meet 'Smartie' and to enjoy his warm friendship thereafter. He was a 'railwayman extraordinaire' with his warm and keen sense of humour and bottomless compendium of railway stories, in the telling of which he never faltered in accurately applying the names of the signalmen, drivers and others who figured therein.

According to Sir John Elliot, in a tribute at the time of 'Smartie's' death, 'that lovable character riding on a "Royal", as he customarily did, with mischievous smile and rare wit to match, asked King George VI for his ticket – and got away with it!'

Shortly before his death, in September 1987, I visited him in his retirement home at Lewes, in company with Tim Bolland. 'Smartie' at 97 was immaculately turned out as usual and, with his mind alert as ever, gave us a last, ever to be remembered treat – more of his incomparable railway stories. What a priceless collection they would have made had he committed them to paper!

'Smartie', as Chief Operating Superintendent, was a tartar for time-keeping throughout the Southern Region and he held routine weekly staff meetings for no other purpose than to investigate timetable lapses. Even 'one minute down' was a serious matter in his estimation. Time was right-time in 'Smartie's' book, and those meetings were no place for the faint-hearted.

It was through 'Smartie' that my railway interest was re-kindled after the war, his kindness providing me with numerous opportunities for travel on the footplate of Bulleid 'Pacifics' out of Waterloo to Weymouth and Exeter. An invitation to travel on the immaculately restored *Swanage* on the Mid-Hants Railway within a week or so of his death made me mindful of him, his kindness and his friendship.

1.
'THE OLD LADY'

In 1958 I was in the employ of John Mowlem & Co as Manager of their Works just south of Hatfield on the East Coast Main Line. A private siding on the down side connected the Works to the main line from a point at the rear of Marshmoor signal cabin, thence climbing a 1 in 60 gradient to the Works entrance and sidings beyond.

Works traffic was handled by two saddle-tank locomotives, a Hudswell Clarke 0-6-0 *London John* and an Andrew Barclay 0-4-0 *Shirley*, these being the last two of a previously large fleet of steam locomotives operated by the company.

As a Reservist I was still required to undergo regular sea-training, and on one of a number of occasions I found myself Engineer Officer of a support ship, HMS *Blackburn*, under the command of Captain W. S. Dobson VRD, RNR. He was an old friend who had previously visited Marshmoor and enjoyed an hour or so on the footplate of the two shunters. On this particular evening, whilst steaming off the west coast of Scotland, we were enjoying a quiet chat on the bridge when inevitably the subject of railways came up. We agreed that they would never be the same for us once the

Marshmoor, south of Hatfield of the East Coast Main Line. Gresley 'A3' 'Pacific' No 60110 *Robert the Devil* passes Marshmoor signal box with a down express. In the right background is Marshmoor BR yard, and in the right foreground the line at the foot of the gradient to Mowlem's sidings, protected by 'traps'. (P. N. *Townend*)

The Marshmoor residents in 1959: Hudswell Clarke 0-6-0 *London John* (with Driver 'Nobby' Smith talking to Colin Morris), and Andrew Barclay 0-4-0 *Shirley*. (*P. N. Townend, R. C. Riley*)

rapidly increasing number of diesel engines brought about removal of all steam engines from the system.

To my amazement, he suggested that it was up to me 'to do my bit for posterity' by securing a steam engine from BR and preserving it in running order. What a marvellous idea! The seed was sown and from that point on my headaches from pondering the method of acquisition and subsequent care of an engine were both numerous and varied.

As a private siding operator, I had come into contact with Geoffrey Huskisson, the Line Manager at King's Cross, and Colin Morris, the District Traction Engineer. Colin was a man to whom I took an immediate liking. He was a practical railwayman and to those who knew him he revealed a nice dry sense of humour. I was fortunate in striking up a close friendship with him, and through his kindness enjoyed many footplate trips on the GN main line with its miscellany of first-class Gresley 'Pacific', 'V2' and 'K3' locomotives, many of which were superbly maintained at Top Shed, where Peter Townend was in charge as Shedmaster.

Colin knew of my addiction to the GN section and its locomotives, but time was beginning to run out and steam turns were rapidly being taken over by the newly introduced diesels which I did my utmost to avoid, in spite of Colin's repeated suggestion that it was time for me to 'make the change'.

On one memorable occasion, I was seeking to ride from King's Cross to Newcastle and he warned me that the train I had suggested had become a 'Deltic' diagram. I duly arrived at King's Cross and waited at the platform end for the engine to come 'off shed'. The route indicator eventually showed that the road had been set for the platform upon which I was waiting. To my amazement, black smoke commenced to spill from the tunnel mouth, not the grey/blue 'Deltic' variety. Very shortly thereafter, I heard a short steam chime whistle and an 'A4' tender-end emerged. When the locomotive finally came within range to permit identification, it proved to be Gresley 'A4' 'Pacific' No 60022 *Mallard*. I had a hard job to hold back tears of both joy and emotion. That proved to be my last steam trip on a BR engine on the GN main line and certainly one of the last that *Mallard* was to make in BR service. It

No 60022 **Mallard** passing Finsbury Park with the down 'Elizabethan'. (*P. N. Townend*)

was an unforgettable experience and that superb engine rode just like a feather-bed!

How could I adequately express thanks to Colin for pulling that one 'out of the bag' for me? When I next saw him and renewed my thanks for his having 're-arranged' things, he was customarily honest and said that he was able to do so only with the co-operation of the crew. He told me that the crew involved were King's Cross men who, warned the day beforehand, had come suitably prepared to work a steam turn. Had the rostered crew been Newcastle men, they would have refused to take *Mallard* since, having worked a diesel up to King's Cross, they would insist upon working a diesel home, or expect to ride 'on the cushions'.

Little did I imagine that nearly 25 years later, at the 10th Anniversary celebrations of the opening of the National Railway Museum at York, I would have the privilege of 'having hold' of that remarkable engine and being able to work her to and fro in the yard for an hour or so.

Reverting to the 'Deltic' locomotive for a moment. It does not seem to be generally known that the 'Deltic' power unit was developed by Rear Admiral (E) W. G. Cowland, Royal Navy, under whom I had

the pleasure of serving as a Lieutenant Commander (E) for a period prior to his retirement in June 1945. He was the only Naval Officer I ever met who wore a grey reefer jacket, achieved through uninterrupted day-long chain-smoking and 'puffing' which showered him – and all present – with 'fag ash'. The diesel engine 'Geoff' developed was originally intended for use in Naval vessels to provide power for generators and other auxiliary equipment (not propulsion). Upon his retirement, he joined the Board of D. Napier & Sons of Acton, part of the English Electric Group of Companies, by whom the engine was adapted for service in railway locomotives.

Meanwhile I continued to give thought to Bill Dobson's suggestion that I should acquire a locomotive. The 'disposals' organisation at Derby had not yet been set up, and in any event I wanted to be selective. The engine had to be an Ivatt or, failing that, a class which had worked on the GN section. To acquire a GN engine I had, of course, to make contact with someone closely involved with them, and the obvious choice was that good friend Colin Morris.

No sooner had I reached that conclusion than I realised that to write to Colin on such

The blue prototype 'Deltic' waiting to leave King's Cross for Doncaster in 1962. (*P. N. Townend*)

a matter could imply discourtesy to his Line Manager. And so, in the autumn of 1958, I took the bull by the horns and prepared and sent a carefully worded letter to Geoffrey Huskisson. Obviously, such an unusual and unprecedented request could hardly bring forth a prompt response, particularly if the outcome was to be in any sense favourable. But I must confess that after six weeks of waiting without any response whatsoever, I had become resigned to failure.

Nevertheless, the telephone in my office rang one morning and the operator announced that it was 'Mr Morris calling from Great Northern House'. We exchanged pleasantries as usual until Colin eventually got round to it.

'Bill,' he said, 'I wanted to speak to you about this letter you've written to Geoffrey. It has caused a bit of a stir here and has been passed from one to another round the office because, you see, BR have never sold an engine before, so no one knows how to go about it!'

Naturally I felt rather uncomfortable at the thought of causing embarrassment to such good friends. However, it was arranged that I meet them at the Great Northern Hotel where, as Geoffrey Huskisson put it, 'you might find it easier to tell me and my colleagues over lunch what you have in mind!'

Accordingly we met at lunchtime one day during the following week where, after a glass of sherry, we shared an enjoyable lunch and 'railway' conversation. But not one word was mentioned about purchase of a steam locomotive until, over coffee, Geoffrey asked why I wanted a locomotive and what I intended doing with it. I replied that I wanted 'to restore it to its original livery and maintain it in working order so that small boys in the future would be able to experience the thrill and enjoyment which steam engines had given to me when I was young'. The Line Manager was a keen and efficient railwayman, but I was aware that he did not possess a 'feel' for motive power and was left with the impression that my case had had little effect upon him.

However, so that they could get back to their desks and continue to 'run the railway' and forget me and my crazy schemes for a while, he suggested to Colin Morris that he take me to the shed for a look round to 'see if you can find anything'. A visit to the Shed at King's Cross was always a special treat, but with Colin as escort and guide it was that day very special indeed, and I was in high spirits as we set off 'to see what we could find'.

As usual there was string upon string of some of the most beautiful engines in the world. Almost without exception they were immaculate, typical of the care and industry of that dedicated and capable Shedmaster, Peter Townend, and his small but equally dedicated depot team. Any less well-turned-out giant was, by its very appearance, a 'visitor'.

Many were, of course, old friends known both by name and number and, in some cases, from footplate acquaintance, and as they towered above us I began to have serious thoughts about possible ownership, size of accommodation to house one, and coal consumption for steam-raising alone. It was a wonderful but frightening world of make-believe.

Turning to the right, Colin 'steered' me to a point where stood the Shed Pilot, an Ivatt 'J52' 0-6-0ST No 68846 in BR black livery, spick and span and, though in steam, quite unattended.

'How about this one, Bill?' said Colin, knowing of my preference for an Ivatt.

Understandably, still heady from the close proximity of the more glamorous and exciting express locomotives, I replied that it didn't really appeal to me, so Colin led me back to 'the more exciting things'.

Some ten minutes or so later, Colin had deftly 'steered' me back until we were once more alongside the 'J52'. Telling me that she was affectionately known as 'the Old Lady' on the shed, he began listing her virtues. Built in 1899, she had seen 60 years of active railway life with the GNR, LNER and latterly BR, had been 'shopped' within the past year, so was in first-class order, was

'Colin steered me to a point where stood the Shed Pilot, Ivatt "J52" 0-6-0ST No 68846, in BR black livery, spick and span and, though in steam, quite unattended...' (P. N. *Townend*)

economical to raise and maintain in steam, not too big to house, not too heavy when faced with repair, and she was one of the last two Ivatts remaining – the other being a completely unserviceable Class 'C12' 4-4-2T No 67352. Due for replacement by a diesel within the next six weeks, the 'J52' might prove to be a relatively easy 'disposal by sale' prospect.

'No harm done by having a look at her, Bill. Let's get on the footplate,' he went on.

That was his master-stroke and, getting the feel of things and considerably more enthusiastic as I became fired with the possibility of ownership, I quickly realised that here was an engine more readily manageable in private ownership than her more glamorous shed-mates. After a thorough look round the clean and tidy cab with the engine humming as sweetly as a kettle as she rested in light steam, I eventually said, 'Well Colin, if this is your recommendation, it's "the Old Lady" for me, please.'

Being told that he would endeavour to process my letter, with No 68846 in mind, but warning that the decision might not be very quickly achieved, we made our way out of the Shed and I caught a train back to Hatfield.

Before leaving Colin that day, I had learned more of the 'immaculate' Ivatt 'C12' No 67352. Her beauty was only skin-deep and she was used solely for exhibition purposes in the King's Cross area, accompanied and hauled by 'J52' No 68846. Indeed, the mechanical condition of the 'C12' was such that she could not be steamed. To add a touch of realism to her appearance when on display, some oily waste was frequently burned in the smokebox!

In his railway masterpiece *Top Shed*, Peter Townend tells how these two locomotives came to be repainted to such an unusually high standard. It was as a result of the Borough of Wood Green celebrating its 750th Anniversary, when BR decided to support the occasion by putting on a Railway Exhibition in Noel Park Yard. In the popular steam section of the Exhibition, *Mallard* 'in steam' was understandably the centre of attraction, supported by Class '9F' No 92196 and the two Ivatts, 67352 and 68846.

The standard of finish of the 'J52' was particularly high and reflected great credit on a depleted Hornsey Loco staff who had produced it out of a shabby, grime-covered shunting engine. Peter goes on to reveal how, when the Exhibition closed, the smart

A further view of 'the Old Lady' as Shed Pilot at King's Cross. (*P. N. Townend*)

The Borough of Wood Green's 750th Anniversary celebrations: young 'drivers to be' get acquainted with 68846 and equally immaculate but unsteamable 'C12' No 67352. (*P. N. Townend*)

'J52' was the subject of a request by Top Shed that she be transferred there from Hornsey in the role of Shed Pilot. What a fortunate transfer that was to prove!

The Class 'J52' saddle tank locomotives were designed by H. A. Ivatt for the Great Northern Railway and Works No 4492 (GNR No 1247, LNER No 4247, BR No 68846) was built by Sharp Stewart & Co in their Atlas Works in Glasgow in 1899, the year which saw the outbreak of the Boer War and invention of the aspirin. With 4 ft 8 in wheels, 18 in x 26 in cylinders and a working boiler pressure of 170 lbs per sq in, these locomotives weighed 52 tons and developed a tractive effort of 21,735 lbs. A total of 129 of the class were built as shunting tanks, but in practice regularly worked 'exchange' and local coal and freight 'trips'. In the south they were to be seen daily, working South London freight trains from Ferme Park to Hither Green, and empty coaching stock in and out of King's Cross terminus.

The men who drove and fired them and worked in the yards beside them were a hardy breed. The engines produced versatility and high productivity unmatched by the BR diesel shunter of today with its vastly reduced work-load. At peak holiday times, 'J52s' were to be seen assisting with empty coaching stock movements between King's Cross and the North London carriage sidings, and to witness one of these locomotives bravely tackling the heavy gradients to Holloway with 60 pairs of wheels unassisted was a never-to-be-forgotten experience.

They were, however, not a popular engine with footplate crews at the beginning of the century and became known as 'starvers' because of their greater work capacity than their predecessors, resulting in less work for drivers and firemen. Usually dirty and uncared-for in appearance, they produced that unmistakable Ivatt throaty and asthmatic 'bark', their work capability being reflected in the large number that were built.

Redundancies among drivers and firemen thus followed hard on the heels of the delivery of the class from the builders at the turn of the century. But once the spectre of unemployment disappeared, crews settled

Contrasts at Hornsey MPD in 1958: 'J52' No 68824, in typically 'hard-worked' state (with a gleaming 68846 in the background), and 68846 as smartened up for the Noel Park Exhibition. (*R. C. Riley, T. S. Greaves*)

'J52' No 68847 at Doncaster on 29 September 1954 with a typical working. (*Major E .A. S. Cotton*)

down to appreciate the new gutsy and spirited tank engines in their charge.

Their duties at that time have to be viewed against the background of the enormous wagon-handling commitment of the Great Northern Railway in the many freight yards which punctuated the whole of their system. This large class of 129 locomotives was fully employed, round the clock, upon the commitment to receive, reform and forward the enormous single-wagon loads of coal, oil, steel and general merchandise which the railways handled at that time, amounting to many thousands of wagon units per day.

The work was continuous and hard and had to be performed with unceasing urgency. Freight trains arriving at regular and frequent intervals had to be split and marshalled to connect with onward freight train diagrams to their ultimate destinations. Failure to keep the flow of wagons moving resulted in choked yards, missed connections, delay in reaching destinations, and frustrating wagon 'losses'.

The importance of the work which these locomotives performed cannot be too highly stressed. Less hardy, versatile and 'work-

hungry' machines could not have survived the constant demands made upon them. Their crews, with never a moment to attempt cleaning care, came to appreciate their worth and the relationship which grew up between them developed into a deep affection.

In the interval between my visit to Top Shed with Colin Morris and definite news from BR, I had of necessity to ponder the problems of locomotive ownership which naturally began to cast their shadows before them. Each step I would soon have to take would be the first by a private individual in the field of steam locomotive restoration, care and, I hoped, operation.

Although it still might never happen, I had to make tentative plans for that exciting possibility. I had one great advantage over many who, it transpired, would later follow in my footsteps. I had access at Marshmoor to a two-road engine shed, equipped to house and already maintaining two working steam locomotives, albeit relatively small industrials. I checked and found that Andrew Barclay 0-4-0 *Shirley* and Hunslet 0-6-0 *London John* would fit snugly into one road, whilst the other was more than adequate for a 'J52'. That was encouraging, but ability to fit 'the Old Lady' into that shed was one thing, approval to do so was something rather different.

My period of employment with the Mowlem organisation in their various Plant depots, whilst rewarding and interesting, had not been by any means the happiest period of my life. I had been singled out for a series of somewhat unpleasant appointments, all concerned with streamlining operations and achieving staff reductions, and my popularity was understandably at no very high level when appointed Manager at Marshmoor. However, I had always enjoyed and valued the confidence and support of Mr E. C. Beck (now Sir Edgar Beck), the Chairman and Managing Director, and when next visiting Head Office in London, I asked for an appointment to see him.

My visits to his office were always a pleasure for me since I had found in him a man who would make a decision and stick to it – there was never requirement for written confirmation of an instruction or his approval. I well remember his smile and greeting that day as he pointed me to a chair.

'Well, Smith, what is it you're after today?'

I believe he must have sensed my less than usual confidence as I gently led up to the 'crunch' of my request to be allowed to keep an engine at Marshmoor. However, his smile widened as he said, 'Good Heavens, Smith, a railway engine, whatever will you be up to next? But of course you may, but do be careful!'

That was the first hurdle cleared, but the course would be long and I realised that there would be many other problems, not always so easily soluble by a friend. But of course I hadn't got an engine yet, merely the hope that one day I might have.

Time passed with still no news, which could only be good news. In the absence of a refusal, the prospects must still be potentially good. Christmas came and went and we were into 1959, and it was not until early March that a telephone call from Colin Morris revealed that No 68846 was still at Top Shed, and if I was still resolved to preserve her, a letter would be prepared and sent to me quite shortly.

That letter, over the signature of Gerry Fiennes, the Line Traffic Manager at King's Cross, was dated 25 March 1959 and reached me the following day. It proved to be the first step into the field of private steam locomotive preservation. The sale price was a particularly reasonable one, which I readily accepted. That sale price I have always treated as a highly confidential matter and, although I have many times been tackled on the subject, I have always refused to disclose it, even to members of my family.

Sometime later I learned that at about this time 'the Old Lady' was struck rather forcefully in the rear by 'something big and heavy' at Top Shed and sustained a fractured rear buffer-beam. With the imminent transfer of ownership, the incident caused a few ripples in that efficient and well-ordered establishment.

Many railway shop floors were constructed of oak wagon headstocks and a suitable piece of timber was obtained from the Wagon Shop at Peterborough, carefully machined and fitted to 68846 to rectify the damage. It was the practice when building earlier locomotives to equip them with wooden buffer-beams with steel facings. No metal facings were fitted to the beam provided in the repair of the 'J52', but the beam has continued to give satisfactory service to this day. Had the 'J52' not been 'sold', this mishap could well have signalled the issue of a one-way ticket to Barry – a narrow escape if ever there was one!

It was decided that the locomotive would work a train from King's Cross to Marshmoor and the hand-over be effected in the BR yard there on Thursday 7 May 1959 (Ascension Day). This is still a day I enjoy celebrating with Peter Townend and is usually marked by my sending him a 'birth-

B.R. 14301/448

BRITISH TRANSPORT COMMISSION

G. F. FIENNES
Line Traffic Manager
J. HANCOCK
Commercial Superintendent
S. D. WARD
Movement Superintendent
C. G. PALMER
Motive Power Officer
Telephone
TERMINUS 3677
Extension
Telegraphic Address
NORTRAF, NORTHLIN
LONDON TASN

Our Reference →
Your Reference

BRITISH RAILWAYS   EASTERN REGION

LINE TRAFFIC MANAGER

(GREAT NORTHERN)

GREAT NORTHERN HOUSE

79/81 EUSTON ROAD

LONDON, N.W.1

25th March 1959.

W. G. Smith, Esq.,
Works Manager,
John Mowlem & Co. Ltd.,
Marshmoor Sidings,
HATFIELD,
Herts.

Dear Mr. Smith,

      I am very glad to have seen over the past few weeks the progress of your plan for keeping a Great Northern locomotive at Marshmoor, and I am very happy to know that the arrangements which we can make have been put to you over the telephone and are acceptable.

      May I confirm the broad heads of the agreement:-

1.   That the locomotive shall be a J.52.

2.   That there shall be a nominal charge to you of £▮▮▮▮

3.   That if in the future you or your assigns wish to dispose of it by sale, you will offer it first back to the Eastern Region at the same price.

4.   That if you propose to scrap the locomotive you will sell it back to us at the same price.

      May I have a brief note from you confirming the arrangements and saying whether there are any particular preferences which you have about the manner in which we should work the engine to you?

      Yours sincerely,

G.F. Fiennes.

day greeting', sometimes in the form of a picture postcard of 1247.

It was suggested that I could join the train at King's Cross for the journey out to Hertfordshire and bring two friends with me. Two, with an interest in railways, immediately sprang to mind and were invited – Kenneth Duke, a well-known Hertfordshire farmer, and Jack Pollitt, both colleagues from my days in the Royal Navy. It was an uncle of the latter who, as a railway constructor many years before, was responsible for building the Great Central line out of Marylebone.

The party, comprising Geoffrey Huskisson, Geoffrey Wright, Colin Morris, Peter Townend, my two guests and myself, were greeted on Platform 13 by Station Master Bill Slater. It is not often that the Station Master at King's Cross puts on his topper and tail-coat, but he did so on Thursday 7 May 1959, and proceeded to Platform 13, setting the travelling public speculating as to the identity of the expected VIP passenger. But the VIP that day was not in *Who's Who* – Bill Slater had put on his topper for 60-year-old Ivatt 'J52' saddle tank No 68846.

There she stood, immaculate and in all

Platform 13, King's Cross station, 7 May 1959. No 68846 waits with the 11.25 'special', and posing proudly in front are Station Master Bill Slater, complete with tail-coat and topper, myself and Peter Townend. (*P. N. Townend, K. D. Duke*)

BRITISH TRANSPORT COMMISSION
British Railways – Eastern Region

TRAFFIC MANAGER,
GREAT NORTHERN HOUSE,
KING'S CROSS

5th May , 1959.

K.P. 1/5183/Pad. 2

Station Master/Shed Master/Yard Master

OFFICERS' SPECIALS.
THURSDAY, 7TH MAY, 1959.
Special trains formed of engine, Saloon 942090 and BSK will run as under:-

Class		'A'	
		a.m.	
King's Cross	dep.	11.25	Platform 13.
		SL	
Potters Bar	pass	11/51	
Marshmoor	arr.	11.58	

To shunt to Sidings.

Class		'A'	
		p.m.	
Marshmoor	dep.	3.15	
		FL	
Potters Bar	pass	3/22	
King's Cross	arr.	3.50	Platform 2.

Light engine to work return special runs as under:-

		p.m.
Hatfield	dep.	2//45
Marshmoor	arr.	2//50

Stations and Depots to acknowledge receipt immediately to Traffic Manager, King's Cross, thus:- "K.P. 1/5183/Pad. 2"

G. F. HUSKISSON,
TRAFFIC MANAGER.

The original of this momentous first Special Traffic Notice for No 68846 has 'Mr Smith's Special' handwritten across the top.

the pride of the occasion at the head of the two-coach special comprising the Line Manager's Saloon and a BSK (brake 2nd composite). What a fantastic change of direction the occasion provided in the life of that vintage locomotive! Off to honourable retirement instead of following in the doomed footsteps of so many other less aged steam locomotives – to the breaker's yard.

As train time of 11.25 approached, the party proceeded to entrain, but my access to the Saloon was barred and I was told by Colin that I had an engine now, and the place for me was on the footplate.

Peter Townend, obviously privy to the arrangements, ushered me forward, followed me up on to the footplate and effected introductions to the crew. To my shame, I cannot recall the name of the driver and fireman on that auspicious occasion, but I do clearly remember that they were two very smartly turned-out young men, obviously hand-picked for the job.

The 'board' came off, the guard gave a green flag and Bill Slater slightly lifted his hat as, with a dignity befitting such an occasion, 'the Old Lady' swept regally out of King's Cross and into Gas Works Tunnel. Could it have been that she simply could

not miss such a golden opportunity to show that the role of pilot at Top Shed had been beneath her station and capability? Fussily she swept past Belle Isle and into Copenhagen Tunnel.

Somewhat to the surprise of both Peter and the driver, we ran 'fast road' to Potters Bar before being turned on to the 'slow' through to Brookmans Park, preparatory to setting back into the yard at Marshmoor. The little engine had all the appearance of thoroughly enjoying the importance of the occasion and of having been allowed 'off shed' on to the main line. We hared along the 'fast road' ahead of the 'Queen of Scots' Pullman following closely upon our heels.

The photograph taken by Tommy Greaves (at that time Shedmaster of the Diesel Depot at Hornsey) from the foot of Hornsey Up signal box always seems to me to convey the spirit of the occasion and suggests an awareness on the part of 68846 that 'something fast is coming up behind'. The hand-over of the 'J52' had been a well-kept secret and I do not recall seeing any lineside photographers that day, which means that his photograph is probably the last taken of the engine in BR ownership.

Marshmoor was reached, the 'special' set

Tommy Greaves's photograph of the 'hand-over special' on the down fast road passing Hornsey Up signal box, 7 May 1959. (T. S. Greaves)

back into the yard and the party de-trained to enjoy the spring sunshine. However, Colin Morris voiced his opinion that a coal-yard was no place in which to mark 'an official handing over of such importance', and proceeded to walk up the access road to the Mowlem private sidings, inspecting the track as he went. He returned shortly to express the opinion that it seemed to him to be in 'quite as good shape as our slow road, so why not take the train up into Mowlem's yard and hand the engine over in more pleasant surroundings?' Slowly others warmed to his suggestion, the party entrained once more, I returned to the foot-plate and the 'special' climbed the 1 in 60 approach and entered the Works sidings to a point of greater privacy – to the amazement of the Works staff! It was the first and only occasion a passenger train entered that yard.

In my letter to Gerry Fiennes accepting his offer of sale of the locomotive, I had promised to make it available for use by BR after restoration, for exhibitions or other occasions when they might have a use for it. Imagine my surprise when, over lunch, Geoffrey Huskisson announced that the new freight depot at New England was to be opened in July and that the appearance of the 'J52' would be a help. Little realising at that point the enormity of the task of restoration to be accomplished in ten weeks, I replied, 'If you would like her at Peterborough, she'll be ready'.

After a most enjoyable and entertaining lunch in the Saloon, the 60 continuous years of railway service of No 68846 with the GNR, LNER, and BR came to an end. Standing beside the locomotive, Colin, in his quiet but jovial way, handed the engine into my keeping with a warm handshake. I was utterly overwhelmed and at that point it was impossible for me to foresee what lay ahead for the locomotive now in my keeping. Suffice it to say that I was acutely aware that so much had to be done before she could have any future whatsoever.

As lunch was ending, I had noticed a Gresley Class 'N2' No 69593, shedded at Hatfield, pass on the up slow road, the crew paying more than passing attention to the 'special' of which they had an excellent view. Being Hatfield men, they obviously knew that something unusual had brought a

The 'special' sets back from the down slow line into the BR yard at Marshmoor, then stands (above right) awaiting the decision to proceed into Mowlem's sidings. Geoffrey Huskisson and Colin Morris stand with their backs to the camera. (P. N. *Townend*)

'special' to Marshmoor and had, into the bargain, proceeded into the private siding. After an interval of 20 minutes or so, we were surprised when the 'N2' slowly climbed the gradient into the yard and buffered up to the Saloon, the driver appearing to have made his own decision that, where an Ivatt 'J52' could go, a Gresley 'N2' can surely

follow. He had come to retrieve the 'special', take it back on to BR metals and work it to King's Cross.

That was the end of a perfect day. Everything from then on was to be through uncharted waters – no one had ever sailed this way before. No 68846 had to be worked carefully through a 180-degree curve in order

'It's all yours!' Colin Morris hands over No 68846 to me at Marshmoor, 7 May 1959. (P. N. *Townend*)

Hatfield 'N2' No 69593 buffers up to the 'special' in Marshmoor yard prior to working the stock back to King's Cross. (P. N. _Townend_)

to enter the Loco in which her road was ready vacated and prepared. This was to be the first of many slow, cautious traversings of that very tight curve, always previously and generously oiled whenever we entered or left the Loco.

Eventually the engine could be 'disposed'

and what was left of that day given over to programming 'restoration', which simply had to start immediately because of that mid-July commitment at Peterborough. If we failed to meet that critical deadline, our credibility with BR would be gone for good – without a shot being fired!

2.
RESTORATION

In common with many Ivatt and early Gresley locomotives, No 68846 had been fitted with bunker rails to increase her coal-carrying capacity and thus her work range, but these did not feature in the original design when Works No 4492 was built by Sharp Stewart of Glasgow in 1899. Thus an early job was to remove the rails together with the cast numberplate from the smokebox door. The locomotive, 'shopped' a year earlier in 1958, was in first-class mechanical order and this meant that stripping of the paint down to the base metal could proceed immediately.

With a view to obtaining guidance in the matter of the many colours which constituted the original GNR livery, I contacted Bob Hunter at the Queen Street Railway Museum at York. He was most helpful in providing letter and numeral specimens of the GNR three-dimensional style of lettering with the aid of which I was able to prepare tracings of the size of letter required. Bob was similarly helpful in obtaining from the Chief Mechanical & Electrical Engineer a drawing of the original 'J52' 'lining out', but could not give me accurate GNR paint shade details.

The paint on the saddle of the engine proved to be relatively thin, but on the bunker, frames, wheels and buffer-beams it was layered up to a thickness in places of $1/8$ in. By careful removal, it was possible to identify the colours previously worn, in turn, by the locomotive during its life, but my

colour-sense is lacking in that 'colour matching' is beyond me, so professional help was needed.

At that time, Goodlass Wall and Co were marketing a range of heat-resistant paints under the trade-name of 'Valspar', and their advertisement depicted a kettle of boiling water being poured over paintwork which they claimed sustained no damage. This association of ideas led me to contact the company at its London office where Mr H. E. Parker was exceedingly helpful in arranging for his Colour Artist to visit Marshmoor to examine the original layers of paint still adhering to parts of the locomotive. The many critical shades were quickly and accurately identified and matched with the extensive range of Valspar lacquer. The company were of further material help in offering to supply the paints required at a most generous level of discount.

Hours of rubbing down were followed by application of a heat-resistant red-lead-based primer before 'panels' of the selected Valspar were applied in readiness for lining-out and lettering. In this work, the support of Peter Murphy, the Foreman Painter at Marsh-moor, was invaluable. Without his patience and helpful advice, the job might well have been an utter disaster.

The locomotive could not be lit up without adequate insurance cover, an important prerequisite whenever pressure vessels are involved. Consequently I needed to discuss the subject fully with qualified

Insurers. Recalling that much of the pressure vessel insurance of the Mowlem Group of Companies was carried by Scottish Boiler and General Insurance Co of Glasgow, I allowed time during my next visit to the Scottish Plant depot at Renfrew to pay a call to their St Vincent Street Office in Glasgow where I was fortunate to secure an interview with the Chief Engineer, Mr T. H. Dunsmoir.

The interview was initially somewhat awkward, due no doubt to the appearance in his office of a potential client with a full-size steam railway locomotive in his backyard. Once he had recovered from his surprise and learned that it had been built in 1899 by Sharp Stewart & Co of Glasgow, his interest was sharpened and our conversation on steam locomotives in general was a very pleasant one, although there is no doubt that he was a devotee of the LNWR.

He eventually proceeded to compile a list of risks for which every responsible locomotive owner must have adequate cover. Of course, all Station Masters have a cat fully entitled to be protected, but did all vicars have their glass-houses built alongside railway lines where an exploding boiler could create havoc? He was painstakingly thorough and when his list was complete, I was quite sure of two things. If a risk was not on Mr Dunsmoir's list, it did not exist, and it was all going to cost a packet! The answer was very quickly forthcoming – a hefty four-figure sum. The shock was sufficient for me to have thoughts of writing to Gerry Fiennes to ask if he would please buy back his 'J52' – and there would be no charge for the painting!

Consternation must have been written all over my face, but Mr Dunsmoir, having enjoyed his moment of high drama, proceeded to lift me gently off the hook with a series of questions, each one more helpful than its predecessor. How often will it be steamed? Not every day of course! When steamed, for how many hours each day, etc, etc... After my answer to each of his many questions, he looked down at his sheet and made a careful calculation. For my part, he

could have questioned me all night because I sensed that every one of his questions was saving me money, faster than I could earn it.

Eventually, with his sheet of paper covered with notes and calculations, he said he believed that they could offer adequate cover of all foreseeable and reasonable risks 'at a very modest figure', subject to a satisfactory report from his local Inspector after inspection of the boiler which, he insisted, must be a thorough inspection. Subject to receiving a satisfactory report, his Agency Manager would proceed to prepare the policy document.

The inspection was eventually carried out at Marshmoor by Scottish Boiler Inspector Mr Merry, from Winslow in Buckinghamshire, on 23 June 1959. Shortly afterwards, I received a letter from the London office of Scottish Boiler informing me that consequent upon the satisfactory examination and test by their Inspector, they would provide cover for the boiler at a premium of £21.1.9d and, in view of the special circumstances relating to its use, would allow 'a return of premium', reducing the nett amount payable to £5.10.0. That night prayers were offered up for all at Scottish Boiler and especially kind and helpful Mr Dunsmoir. Such is the efficacy of prayer that when the policy eventually reached me on 14 August 1959, the accompanying account amounted to only £4.14.6d, convincing me that preservation of 1247 was moving along nicely in the right direction, with a gently following wind.

Meanwhile, with the material support of Goodlass Wall, the repainting had reached a point where the panels were ready and awaiting lining-out and lettering, and it was patently obvious that a critical stage had been reached where specialist help was again needed.

Speaking of this on the telephone to Peter Townend, I nervously asked if he thought his Foreman Painter at Top Shed, Fred Raynor, would be willing to give a hand one weekend. Peter undertook to have a word with Fred and, after a day or so, phoned to say that he had agreed to travel out on the

SCOTTISH BOILER AND GENERAL INSURANCE COMPANY LTD

ESTABLISHED 1881

TELEPHONE
METropolitan 6242.

BECKET HOUSE,
36/37 OLD JEWRY,
LONDON, E.C.2

Your Ref:

Our Ref: LN/IT.

23rd June, 1959.

W.G. Smith, Esq.,
15, Florence Drive,
Enfield,
Middlesex.

Dear Sir,

Insurance of Loco Boiler.

With reference to your discussions in our Glasgow office regarding the insurance of this Loco Boiler, we now have pleasure in attaching our Engineer Surveyor's Report in connection with the various examinations and tests which he has carried out.

We suggest that the Boiler be insured against explosion risks, including Third Party liability for an indemnity of £100,000 and in addition, the Boiler be insured against over heating. The normal Premium would be £21.1s.9d. and we are preparing a Policy which will be issued showing this Premium. However, in view of the circumstances regarding the use of this Boiler, we are prepared to allow a return of Premium which will reduce the net figure payable to £5.10s.0d. and this return will be dealt with by way of separate Endorsement. The Policy and our account for £5.10s.0d. will be sent to you in due course.

Yours faithfully,
SCOTTISH BOILER AND GENERAL INSURANCE CO: LTD.,

London Manager.

next Saturday morning to line-out and letter the locomotive.

It was arranged that I should meet Fred at Brookmans Park station and take him to Marshmoor. Having met him only once before at Top Shed, I could not claim to know him well, and I was therefore the more anxious that all should be ready, to save time and encroach upon his weekend as little as possible.

Believing that a good sound footing would go far to ensure straight, even lines, I had placed adjustable steel trestles all round the locomotive at running-plate height with scaffold boards, three-wide, upon them, in readiness for Fred's visit. He was a quiet, thoughtful man, and immediately he saw the staging surrounding the engine I sensed, by the expression on his face, that we had a problem. I said that I hoped the staging was to his liking and at the correct height, to which he replied that he would 'not require any staging'!

A rapid 'scene-shifting' exercise removed the offending platforms and Fred then proceeded to extract from his pocket a small

Expert painter Fred Raynor (extreme left) with No 68846 at Top Shed, King's Cross, in 1959. (*P. N. Townend*)

cylindrical container some $1^1/2$ inches in diameter and 5 inches deep and a short paint brush. Removal of the screw cap on the container revealed that it contained white paint and, from closer examination, the 'brush' appeared to have no more than a dozen long, droopy hairs, each approximately 1 inch in length.

Fred appeared satisfied with the chalk lines defining the panels on saddle, cab and bunker which had been set out in accordance with the CM&EE's drawing obtained by Bob Hunter. Clipping the paint container to his breast pocket and placing the brush between his teeth, he climbed on to the running-plate, grasped the handrail with his left hand and got busy with the brush in his right. His work-rate was fantastic, and quickly his straight, even white lines encompassed the engine, putting a finishing touch to the beautiful multi-coloured scheme.

In an amazingly short time, Fred stepped down with the lining-out completed, and I broached the subject of letters and numerals of which I said I had produced full-size

tracings. He replied that he 'wouldn't need tracings' and promptly climbed up and proceeded to chalk and then paint in the letters and numerals with swift confident strokes, just as he had tackled the lining-out. He was a first-class tradesman and a joy to watch. In no time at all the job was beautifully completed and, full of gratitude, I was conveying him back to a train at Brookmans Park.

But how can one adequately express thanks for such kindness? Without generous help such as that, restoration to the standard for which I was striving could never have been achieved. All we needed now was a quiet still spell of weather to seal off the job with three good coats of clear marine varnish – our luck held, and the result was breath-taking! After the final coat had dried, a large water sprinkler was played over the locomotive to 'harden' it off and so reduce the risk of damage during future cleaning operations.

While all this had been going on, I had talked over with Bill Jones, the Yard Foreman, the new role I hoped would be

Two views of No 1247, as she now was, newly restored at Marshmoor, July 1959. (*H. C. Smith, P. N. Townend*)

secured by 1247 – hauling passenger trains on BR. It would obviously be vital to quickly attain and constantly maintain our top speed of about 30 mph to avoid both unpopularity and scorn if our exploits ever caused delay to BR services through failing to keep time. Among Bill's duties was responsibility for the company's steam locos, and he put forward the suggestion that we conceal a mechanical lubricator between the frames to provide added 'front-end' lubrication for the engine in her passenger role. This was the only deviation we indulged in and I believe that the successful manner in which 1247 was later to adapt to passenger working owes much to this small 'deceit'.

3.
EARLY OUTINGS

During the final stages of restoration, which coincided with the rapidly approaching July date of opening of the New England Freight Depot at Peterborough, I had maintained a close liaison with Great Northern House to ensure that after the 'sprint finish' in restoring 1247, we were not 'shut out' through lack of contact. Eventually it was issued and my copy arrived – the prized Special Traffic Notice for us to run 'light' to New England on 1 July 1959. The details are reproduced opposite.

On the day of departure, with a carefully filled bunker of coal, the boiler was filled and a small fire kindled in the firebox. Very shortly the locomotive began to 'sweat' so heavily that I feared not a vestige of paint would remain by the time steam was raised. This was a problem which would have to be faced and overcome in future, but for the present a thorough oil round had to be carried out and the 'bag' dropped in to fill the saddle to capacity with water.

All was complete and 1247 was in light steam by the time I had been told to expect a King's Cross Inspector, Frank Knight, who would check over and pass the engine before we were released on to the main line by Marshmoor box. Frank was a tall, thorough man who never gave the impression of hurrying and was quite unflappable. Working methodically round 1247, he had eyes for everything and insisted upon replacing all the existing lubricating 'trimmings' with a set of his own, produced from his jacket pocket. This proved to be the first of many trips with Frank who was invariably detailed to see that we 'got there and back safely'. He had thought to bring with him, on his soon-to-become familiar motor-cycle combination, a can which, he revealed, contained 'Jubilee Oil'. This, he explained, was a rape oil specially prepared for use by 'Pacifics' on their long non-stop diagrams on the East Coast Main Line – Frank's can was to accompany 1247 everywhere!

In conversation with Peter Townend some years later, I learned that although the percentage of rape additive to lubricating oil is customarily in the region of 5 per cent, it was as high as 25 per cent in the Jubilee Oil.

Surprisingly, it was not adopted by Traction Engineers at Haymarket and Gateshead, but used only at Top Shed. I did not ask if there was any evidence to show that 'Pacifics' on down workings, previously serviced at King's Cross with Jubilee Oil, performed any better than when working up diagrams after servicing in the North with standard BR lubricants. It was possibly a case of Top Shed having built up faith in a product, and I had no lack of that faith – it certainly worked wonders for an obscure shunting engine elevated to passenger train workings.

We were shortly joined by a pair of New England men who had been rostered to work the engine to Peterborough, and then embarked upon a course of footplate discipline which was, as so often in the future, to enable four men to fit into such a small cab,

BRITISH TRANSPORT COMMISSION
British Railways – Eastern Region
Circular No.K.981

MOVEMENT OF LIGHT ENGINE, MARSHMOOR TO NEW ENGLAND
1ST JULY, 1959

A J.52 light engine, travelling at reduced speed, will run as under:-

		p.m.
Marshmoor		12//50
		SL
Hatfield	arr.	1. 0
	dep.	1.30
Digswell		1/x40
		ML
Woolmer Green		1/x45
		SL
Hitchin		2/ 8
Arlesey		2/x25
		SL
Biggleswade		2x47
		ML
Sandy		2/x54
		SL
Huntingdon		3/x23
		ML
Yaxley		3/x57
		GL
Peterborough North		4/x12
New England		4//20

Loco Shed Master, New England, to provide set of men to travel out passenger on 9.12am from Peterborough North (due King's Cross 10.53am) and 11.40am from King's Cross (due Hatfield 12.18pm), proceed to Marshmoor and obtain engine.

All stations and depots to acknowledge receipt of this circular immediately by telegram to "Trafman KF3 King's Cross" thus "K.981".

G. F. HUSKISSON,
TRAFFIC MANAGER.

T.M.O. KING'S CROSS.
29th June, 1959.
M.E.3/9555

yet allowing space for the driver and fireman to work unimpeded.

With a 'right away' from the Marshmoor signalman, we eased out of the yard behind the box and on to the down slow road. It was a moment of high excitement mixed with a great sense of achievement. Although not working a passenger train, or for that matter any train, we had at least achieved modest 'respectability' in being trusted on BR metals – a treasured and proud moment for a privately owned steam locomotive in 1959.

All we had to do was to get to Peterborough and back to Marshmoor without mishap and to avoid delay or annoyance to other traffic.

News of our emergence had not got to the Press and consequently there was a complete absence of the 'Kodak brigade'. Our slow passage, with frequent signal stops, was, however, one of more than usual interest to BR staff *en route*. We certainly proved to be a 'work-stopper' that day. Many of the older signalmen saluted our passing, while more senior PW men 'presented arms' with pick or shovel.

And that was how, in July 1959, a small Ivatt locomotive built in 1899 and with 60 years of continuous railway service behind her, became the first privately owned locomotive permitted to work over BR metals.

Arriving at the new Freight Depot, we were in 'display order', buffered-up to Gresley Class 'A4' No 60022 *Mallard*, our old Top Shedmate.

Although beautifully prepared for display, the 'A4' had not been completely repainted but merely touched-up in the few hours available to Fred Raynor when he was able to get possession of her between diagrams. With 1247 quite resplendent alongside, I felt a deep sense of gratitude to him that, only able to do a quick tidy-up to one of his beautiful Top Shed 'A4s', he had, so generously in his own time, helped to expertly finish 1247 for me.

Reports of the Exhibition, officially opened by Lady Benstead, wife of Sir John Benstead, Deputy Chairman of the British Transport Commission, claimed it to have been 'a great success. Exhibits included the latest diesel locomotive, a diesel train, many specialised types of wagon, examples of the latest 1st and 2nd Class coaches, numerous types of specialised containers for various traffics, *Mallard* and 1247'. It was claimed that on each day of opening, some 9,000 people crossed each steam engine footplate.

1247 makes her first public appearance at the BR Exhibition to mark the opening of the new Freight Depot at New England, Peterborough, in July 1959.

Our transit from Marshmoor to New England had been leisurely, and we covered the journey without the requirement to take water. The return journey, however, was a much different affair as can be seen from the details reproduced below.

The locomotive was in charge of New England Driver Fred Jones, with his Fireman, John Wilkinson. Frank Knight was on leave and King's Cross Inspector Bill Buxton, travelled with us. We were booked to depart New England at 13.40, and the Motive Power report on the trip, reproduced overleaf, reveals considerable running in excess of 30 mph. As will be seen, 6 minutes were lost taking water at Hitchin, but we reached Marshmoor 12 minutes before time and so had got our first job safely completed and under our belt. It was with a great sense of relief that the locomotive was 'disposed' and propelled gently into the shed at Marshmoor by Hunslet 0-6-0 *London John.*

BRITISH TRANSPORT COMMISSION
British Railways – Eastern Region
Circular No.K1009

MOVEMENT OF LIGHT ENGINE, NEW ENGLAND TO MARSHMOOR
20TH JULY, 1959

The J.52 light engine which travelled from Marshmoor to New England on the 1st July (Circular K.981) will return as under:-

	p.m.
New England	1//40
Peterborough North	1/x48
	ML
Connington South	2/x8
	GL
Leys	2/x21
	ML
Huntingdon	2/30
Sandy	2/x55
	SGL
Arlesey	3/x10
	SL
Hitchin	3/22
Woolmer Green	3≠55
Hatfield	4/12
Marshmoor	4//18

Loco Shed Master, New England to provide set of men to work throughout. R.A.R.

All stations and depots to acknowledge receipt of this circular immediately by telegram to "Trafman K.F.3. King's Cross" thus "K.1009".

G. F. HUSKISSON,
TRAFFIC MANAGER.

T.M.O. KING'S CROSS.
14TH JULY, 1959.
K.F.3/9555.

BRITISH TRANSPORT COMMISSION
BRITISH RAILWAYS

Motive Power
Running & Maintenance Dept. *New England* *E* **Region.**

20 · 7 – 1959

Weather *Fine*

REPORT OF INSPECTOR : *W. Buxton* ON THE RUNNING OF THE

1-40 p. m. ~~**Passenger**~~ ~~**Freight**~~ *Light Engine* train from *New England* to *Marshmoor*

on *20 · 7 · 1959*

PASSENGER—
Classification .... Actual tons .... Regulation tons ....

FREIGHT—
Classification .... Actual & Equivalent Wagons .... Regulation Load ....

(1) Driver *J. Jones* Fireman *J. Wilkinson* Depot *New England*

(2) Driver .... Fireman .... Depot ....

(1) Loco. No. *1247* Type & M.P. Class *J52* Depot ....

(2) Loco. No. .... Type & M.P. Class .... Depot ....

STATIONS	BOOKED TIMES		ACTUAL TIMES		MINUTES		CAUSE
	Arr.	Dep.	Arr.	Dep.	Lost	Recovered	
New England		1-40		1-32		8	Early departure
					2		Signals Peterborough
Peterborough	1-48		1-42				
Bennington South	2-8		2-2				
					6		Signals Leys
Leys	2-21		2-21				
						2	By Engine
Huntingdon	2-30		2-28				
						2	By Engine
Sandy	2-55		2-51				
						3	By Engine
Arlesey	3-10		3-3				
					2		Signals Cadwell
Hitchin	3-22		3-17	3-23	6		Taking Water
						1	By Engine
Woolmer Green	3-55		3-47			2	By Engine
Hatfield	4-12		4-2			2	By Engine
Marshmoor	4-18		4-0				

Remarks :— *General condition of Engine Satisfactory.*
Riding and Steaming Satisfactory.
Performance of Enginemen's duties Satisfactory.

Signature *W. Buxton*

Inspector Buxton's Report on the running of 1247 from New England to Marshmoor, 20 July 1959.

The next day after returning from New England saw a careful cleaning of the paintwork in warm water with a sprinkling of soap flakes. Brightwork was cleaned and lightly oiled and a 'lid' placed over the chimney. The July weather was warm and the boiler water was not 'dropped' for three or four days, by which time the temperature had fallen to a point where the residual heat was just sufficient to dry off the tubes and shell as the water level receded.

The crew who had worked 1247 from King's Cross to Marshmoor in May had warned me of one or two points to watch. They pointed out that the Ivatt regulator was prone to easing open when in steam, allowing the engine to move off if not securely braked. I was therefore particularly careful from the start to see that the reversing lever was in 'middle' and the handbrake always hard on before leaving the footplate, even if only for a short period. I also decided to evolve my own set of extra safety precautions, and suspended a small wooden wedge by a cord from the regulator slide bracket with which to wedge the regulator shut. Additionally I obtained some wooden chocks which were invariably placed on either side of the middle pair of wheels – just to make doubly sure!

1247 was a very free running engine and like many small tanks would move on as little as 20 lbs of steam. Stopping her was an entirely different kettle of fish, since there was no effective brake at less than 100 lbs per sq in. With lack of care, it would have been a simple matter to carve a profile of the engine in the end wall of the shed through being tempted to move her inside under light steam, realising all too late that she had insufficient steam to operate the vacuum ejector.

Prominent in my mind was the sweating problem when lighting up, and after discussion with Bill Jones it was decided to introduce a heat-exchanger into the feed-water line in the shed. We had ample steam at our disposal from a central boiler-house, so henceforth the 'J52' was always charged with warm water before lighting up, with the added bonus of reducing the steam-raising time. This effectively overcame the sweating problem and safeguarded the precious livery.

On the outward journey to New England, Frank Knight had emphasised the vital necessity to conserve water at all times. He pointed out that hauling a passenger train would face 1247 with a water requirement every 30 miles. A few years earlier this would have presented no problem, but introduction of the diesel locomotive encouraged BR to quickly take the opportunity of removing every water facility immediately it could be dispensed with. Thus route planning was often determined by water availability – a situation which was to worsen rapidly.

With the first 'sortie' on to BR metals behind us, the next item on the agenda was for me to make a closer acquaintance with the operation and handling of the loco-motive and, for a number of weekends there-after, 1247 was steamed in the sidings at Marshmoor for that express purpose – and for the entertainment and accommodation of visitors.

Costs were relatively light since firing was by the use of conveniently sized sleeper ends with only a sprinkling of coal. This had the advantage of gently scouring the tubes which, in the conditions under which we were operating, never needed cleaning.

The 1 in 60 approach gradient provided an excellent length of straight track, and a couple of tube wagons or bogie-bolsters with brakes pinned partly down gave sufficient of a simulated load to encourage a nice asthmatical bark from 'the Old Lady'. This attracted a goodly muster of photographers from near and far, together with friends and their young who were always invited to savour the excitement of a visit to the footplate of a steam locomotive.

One such visitor, whose name I cannot recall, produced diarised notes recording a visit he paid to Marshmoor on Saturday 19 March 1960. He wrote:

'It was not a particularly brilliant or spring-like day, in fact it was infernally cold, but quite dry for an outside venture by anyone reasonably robust. The day had no special significance and carried no particular comment in the calendar.

'For the writer, however, and a few others "in the know", it was a day reserved for a very special kind of party, as the following paragraphs will relate.

'About 20 miles north of London and alongside the erstwhile LNER King's Cross to Edinburgh main line, is an extremely efficient plant maintenance yard belonging to a well-known firm, equipped with an internal standard gauge rail system, connected to the main line. Traffic on this system is handled by two well-kept industrial saddle tanks, one 0-4-0 and one 0-6-0, both painted (visible) green. Not more than one is usually in steam.

'Here we must come to the main part of these notes. The two little industrial shunters have as stable companion a GNR saddle tank 0-6-0 built by Sharp Stewart & Co, Glasgow, in 1899 to the design of H. A. Ivatt, class "J52" No 1247. She is painted, lined and lettered completely to the old GNR specification, the work having been done by the present owner, the

Yard Manager, whose property she now is. Her appearance is magnificent, and when stored, she is clothed all over with a pale magenta-coloured sheet.

'The flat racing season has now started and undoubtedly with this in view it was decided that the running season for No 1247 should also open, so Saturday 19th March was selected as the opening day. To give the guests, among whom the writer was privileged to be, a good show, all three engines were in steam and the odd quarter-mile of straight road, mostly at an incline of 1 in 60, was given over to running the "favourite". Occasionally the sun came out, albeit rather feebly – but what a fine sight she looked.

'Her running was delightful – valve events were even, and everything including steam brake and injectors seemed to behave well at slightly below 100 lbs per sq in on the gauge, and the whistle gave a satisfactory answering "crow" to blasts from passing enthusiasts on the main line, both steam and diesel. The length of the run allowed for notching-up, although the reversing lever had a very busy time during the many trips made. The only item we did not see in use was the sanding gear, but without a train to haul, and a dry day prevailing, this was not required. The fire was

1247 in Mowlem's yard at Marshmoor. The height of the sidings at the top of the 1 in 60 gradient above the East Coast Main Line beyond can clearly be seen. (H. C. *Smith*)

fed mainly with timber baulks and very little coal, consequently we were virtually smokeless and only white puffs (nostalgic) issued from the chimney.

'It is not easy to express the simple pleasure of standing on top of a spotless apple-green saddle tank holding a water filling pipe (fire-hose) in position. It is equally hard to put into words one's own feelings during the whole day's proceedings, other than to say one wouldn't have missed them for all the tea in China, India and Ceylon too.

'In conclusion, the writer, as a confessed incurable GNR protagonist, must express profound appreciation of the owner's action in procuring this engine, restoring it and maintaining it in operating condition, no mean responsibility and entailing an enormous amount of work, far in excess of what many of us would realise. It is interesting to reflect that if we include the small-boilered "Atlantic" No 990, the large one No 251 and Stirling's famous No 1, there are now four GNR locomo-

tives fully restored and maintained. Perhaps some day, they may all be seen together in steam.

'A word of thanks is written here, which may be seen by the owner, for a day which will never be forgotten. G.B.R.'

One very distinguished visitor who travelled specially to Marshmoor was Sidney W. Smart ('Smartie') to whom reference has earlier been made. He greatly enjoyed his footplate ride as did I his lively, light-hearted company.

An approach was made by the BBC to feature 1247 in their *Tonight* series which would be shot at Marshmoor. On the appointed Sunday, 20 March 1960, the engine was prepared early to allow time for an extra-special polish, as befitted such an occasion. At the appointed time, the film unit arrived and, in beautiful sunshine, we went through the routines they asked for.

These principally comprised running up the bank with the brake partially applied to give a realistic 'bark' and plenty of smoke,

'...there are now four GNR locomotives fully restored and maintained.' GNR 'Atlantic' No 2811 was not one of then, seen here at Doncaster in 1947 awaiting scrapping—although useable parts evidently lived on. (P. N. Townend)

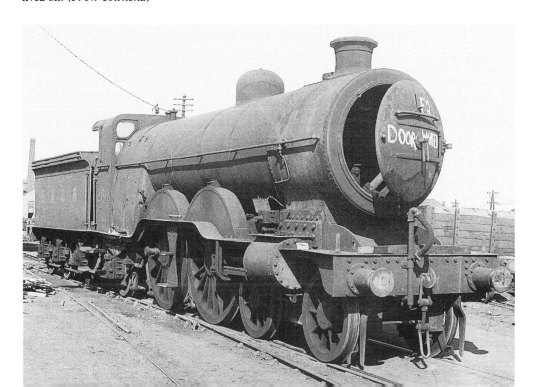

Sidney W. Smart CBE ('Smartie'), Chief Operating Superintendent of BR Southern Region, accompanied by Tim Bolland on a visit to Marshmoor in 1960.

whilst a shooting-brake with roof-mounted camera raced alongside on the parallel roadway. With close-up action shots of the wheels and rods to follow, the time passed quickly, and before long *Tonight's* reporter, Alan Whicker, arrived.

He said that he required us to make another noisy, high-speed run up the bank whilst he would stand with his cameraman at the top of the grade in the centre of the track, in readiness for 'close-ups'. He stated that it would need very accurate stopping, at a point indicated with the toe of his shoe. I picked up a large white stone marker and placed it where he had indicated. Before we set back to the foot of the bank, he said that he wanted me to step down from the left-hand-side footplate steps just before the engine came to rest. I had to tell him that 1247 was right-hand drive, and if he wanted me to dismount from the left-hand side whilst the engine was still in motion, my fireman would have to drive. This secured approval from Mr Whicker although he was most insistent on one point – 'But don't

forget to tell him he must stop at the white stone'.

We set back to the yard gate at the foot of the gradient and with a whistle set off to give a 'display magnificent', with clouds of smoke and full-throated barks from the exhaust. The young BR fireman rose to the occasion beautifully, and I stood at the top of the steps ready to dismount, as directed. Unfortunately, the fireman overshot Mr Whicker's white stone and worked to another, some yards further on. As I stood on the bottom step, I got an excellent view of Mr Whicker diving one way and the camera operator, with tripod and all, going the other! I could not suppress a laugh, but Mr Whicker was not amused! We were sent back down the bank in disgrace – to do it all again. The second approach was spot-on and the interview went 'in the can' without another hitch. Shortly thereafter, the BBC sent the fee of 8 guineas 'for appearing in film story shot'. No mention was made of a long day's work, use of the locomotive and fuel!

CAPT. W. SMITH

TELEVISION (Talks)

THE BRITISH BROADCASTING CORPORATION
Head Office : BROADCASTING HOUSE, LONDON, W.I
TELEVISION CENTRE, WOOD LANE, LONDON, W.12
TELEPHONE : SHEPHERDS BUSH 8030   TELEGRAMS : BROADCASTS, TELEX, LONDON

Our Reference :   35/BH   14th April 1960,

DEAR

With reference to our invitation to you to ~~prepare and deliver a talk~~ *appear* in our television programmes we offer you an engagement on the terms and conditions shown below and overleaf. If you accept, kindly sign and return the attached confirmation sheet, or reply otherwise, as soon as possible. (See condition 1 overleaf.)

Title .... TONIGHT

Date(s) of Recording   Filming 20th March 1960   REHEARSAL(S)

Time(s) of Recording

Place   *Alan Whicker*

Date of First Broadcast   22nd March 1960   *and Peter Batty.*

Time of First Broadcast   6.50 p.m.

Producer   Donald Baverstock.

Fee   Inclusive Eight Guineas (£8. 8. 0.) for appearing in film

         story shot for inclusion in above programme.

Letters addressed to speakers c/o the BBC will be forwarded, but for statistical purposes the letters may be opened before being forwarded unless we are notified of any objection.   Letters marked " Personal " are forwarded unopened.

Capt. W. Smith,   Yours faithfully,
C/o Messrs. John Mowlam & Son,   THE BRITISH BROADCASTING CORPORATION
Welham Green,
Nr. Hatfield,
Hertfordshire.   *Barbara Hunter*

                                          pp. HOLLAND P.
                                          Television Booking Manager

P/412/F 2-59 6000 A.E.B

The following year I received a pleasant surprise in the form of a request from the Stephenson Locomotive Society who had planned a members-only brake-van special along the 'freight only' line from Hatfield to St Albans Abbey and return. They wished 1247 to work their 'special' on Saturday 17 June 1961.

I had earlier decided that if an approach was made for the use of the locomotive it would always be made available without any charge whatsoever, on the understanding that the organisers chartered the stock from BR and obtained authority for us to provide the motive power. This, therefore, was the basis of the agreement with the SLS for their brake-van special, and on all subsequent occasions when 1247 was used. I was quite happy to maintain the engine and provide it for 'charter' excursions – the bonus for the locomotive and myself was the opportunity to get out on to BR metals.

On the appointed day, 'the Old Lady' was prepared and by the time we were in light steam, Frank Knight appeared to carry out his leisurely but thorough inspection, accompanied by his customary can of Jubilee Oil. In good time, we set back down to the rear of Marshmoor box where we were met by Driver Lew Levelrsha and his fireman. They were a young and very pleasant crew, and such was the enthusiasm of the fireman that thereafter he came regularly to Marshmoor when we were steaming the engine in the yard.

We went slow road to Hatfield, were run through the platform and then set back on to the train of eight 'Queen Mary' 'fitted' goods brake-vans which had been placed ready for us. After coupling up and carrying out a brake-test, we were put into the down slow platform to pick up the passengers. The platform was stiff with bodies, cameras held aloft in the only position from which it was possible to take pictures. In due course, travellers extricated themselves from the hoards of platform ticket holders to board the train.

SATURDAY, 17th JUNE						
980. SPECIAL TRAIN						
Class ...	...	...	...	...	...	**B**
						p.m.
Mowlems Siding ...	...	...	...	...	12||A50
Marshmoor	...	...	...	...	...	12 55
Hatfield	...	...	...	...	...	1|| 0
"	...	...	...	...	...	1 45
Hill End	...	...	...	...	...	1 56
St. Albans Abbey	...	...	...	...	2 5
"	...	...	...	...	...	2 20
Hill End	...	...	...	...	...	2 29
Hatfield	...	...	...	...	...	2 40

A.—Class J52 Locomotive
STOCK.— { 8 Fitted Brake Vans.
{ " Stephenson Locomotive Society."

Eastern Region (GN Line) Special Traffic Notice for 17 June 1961.

In charge of the excursion was Inspector C. Redgers from King's Cross who in 1951, whilst on the Hatfield station staff, had attended the departure of the last passenger train to St Albans Abbey. In smart blue suit and with a red rose in his buttonhole, he had

1247 sets back into the platform at Hatfield to load passengers for the SLS brake-van special along the St Albans branch, 17 June 1961. (R. C. Riley)

SLS President Jack Boston passes the time of day with Driver Lew Levelrsha at Hatfield before departure. (*F. Mayo*)

Youthful admirers from St Albans watch Driver Levelrsha take the token for the St Albans branch at Hatfield as 1247 takes water. (*R. C. Riley*)

1247 departs from St Albans Abbey station with the SLS special. (*R. C. Riley*)

earlier taken the precaution of walking the line, clearing debris so that our excursion would not be delayed. At each level crossing we encountered, he climbed down, unlocked and opened the gate, closing and re-securing it after we had passed.

Ronald Biggs wrote in the *Herts Advertiser* of the trip:

'We rocked about on the platform of a brake-van hauled by a Spartan little engine known to members of SLS as GNR No 1247. The engine gleamed and shone in the June sunlight, smoke belched and the whistle blew.

'Wiping away the smuts, we stared watery-eyed at unfamiliar countryside along the single-track branch line between Hatfield and St Albans, closed to passenger traffic since 1951.

'I stood on the heaving platform on the brake-van with the President of the Society, Mr Jack Boston, a builder from Hadley Wood. At his invitation, I took a lungful of what he described as "the most wonderful smell in the world". A mixture of hot oil, smoke and steam.

'The engine, resplendent in its original livery of 1899, stopped with a squeal of

brakes at a level crossing. Enthusiasts not on the train surged across fields and swarmed over bridges, photographing 1247 from all angles.

'All too soon, we were back at Hatfield where we steamed into the station alongside diesel D5057. As a curtain drop, Gresley "A4" "Pacific" No 60021 *Wild Swan* roared through with an up express and those few Society members with another shot left in their cameras, joyfully photographed her.'

For our part, after a short but enjoyable outing, we ran gently back to Marshmoor, and home.

Shortly after the excitement of the brake-van special, I heard from the South Beds Loco Club with a request for 'the Old Lady' to work a charter train they were organising for Saturday 16 September 1961. 'The Lea Flyer' was to work from Welwyn Garden City to Hertford East by way of the 'freight only' line and return thence from Welwyn

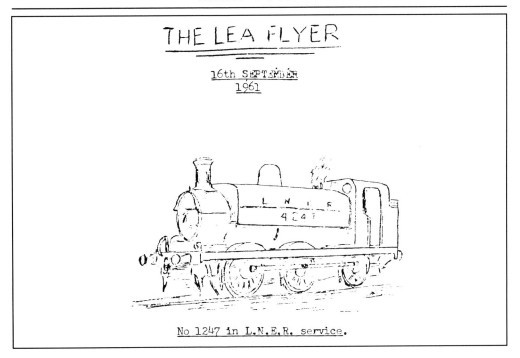

THE LEA FLYER

16th SEPTEMBER
1961

No 1247 in L.N.E.R. service.

A nice sketch of 'the Old Lady' on the cover of 'The Lea Flyer's' itinerary.

2Z10. RAIL TOUR
SOUTH BEDFORDSHIRE LOCOMOTIVE CLUB

	2Z10		3Z10
Class	**B**	Class	**C**
	p.m.		p.m.
Welwyn Garden City	2 15	Luton Bute Street .... *ETY*	6†16
Cole Green	2 37	Harpenden East .... *COACHES*	6 28
	2 50	"	6 42
Hertingfordbury	2 56	Ayot	6 54
"	3 10	Welwyn Garden City	7 0
Hertford Old	3 26	"	7 10
"	4 15	Hatfield	7†18
Welwyn Garden City	4 51		
	SL		
Hatfield	4 56	Class	C *AMENDED*
"	5 15		
Welwyn Garden City	5 21		*pm.*
Ayot	5 27	Waterworks .... *ETY*	2 45 *12·40*
"	5 33	*COACHES*	
Wheathampstead	5 41	Potters Bar	2 55 *1-0*
Harpenden East	5a49	Hatfield	3 5 *1-10*
Luton Bute Street	6 2	Welwyn Garden City	3 10 *1-15*

STOCK AND FORMATION.—Privately-owned Locomotive J.52 0–6–0 (No. 68845), 5 T.S.O., B.S.K.

Passengers to travel outward from Luton Bute Street by **2203** Up due to depart Luton Bute Street **1.32** p.m., Welwyn Garden City arr. **2.0** p.m.

Train crews to operate gates at Attimore, Birchall & Dicker Mill in each direction.

Special Traffic Notice for the 'The Lea Flyer'.

Garden City to Luton (Bute Street) via Wheathampstead and Harpenden (East). Support was envisaged from 300 passengers and the train would comprise a six-car Outer Suburban set – a nice load for a Saturday afternoon meander through the Hertfordshire countryside.

We followed the customary preparation pattern, and Frank Knight appeared, with customary can, and gave his seal of approval. We were joined by Hatfield Driver Charlie Winter and his fireman. Working light to Welwyn Garden City, we picked up the stock there and, with an enthusiastic load of passengers, we departed at 2.15 pm and made our leisurely way through the wooded glades and fields of ripening corn.

The crowds at the lineside and on bridges were thick and enthusiastic of our progress as we approached our first photographic stop at Cole Green, thence on to Hertingfordbury to be warmly greeted by Mr and Mrs George

Flunders who had occupied the Station House for 26 years. George was originally the Hertingfordbury Booking Clerk, but with the closure of the station had moved on to Welwyn Garden City as a Goods Clerk. Mrs Flunders claimed to 'miss the steam trains very much' and had little time for 'dirty, smelly diesels', so our visit pleased her. She recalled the days when their well ran dry and her only supply of water, hot and cold, was from engines calling at the station.

At our next stop, Hertford (East), we met Bill Lawrence, aged 51, the head shunter in Hertford yard. Starting as a porter, he had been with the railway since 1924. Looking back to the days when the yard was shunted by horses, he regaled us with a story of one particularly temperamental old horse who would refuse to work until he had been given three pints of beer. Looking at Bill, it occurred to me that the horse might have acquired the taste from its master!

Making ready to leave Welwyn Garden City with 'The Lea Flyer': myself, the guard and interested spectators. (F. Mayo)

'The Lea Flyer' leaves Welwyn Garden City station for Hertford, 16 September 1961. (*F. Mayo*)

We took water, ran round the train and then retraced our steps to Welwyn Garden City. Negotiating the main line to cross from the up to the down side, we were then able to run-round again and all was ready for an enjoyable run along that most pleasant and picturesque line to Harpenden (East) and Luton (Bute Street). The branch was a favourite of mine in that the farm of my maternal grandparents was on the east side of the line to the north of Harpenden station, from which point I had as a boy regularly observed the trains.

The crowds down the branch were thick and I could only ponder on the growing enthusiastic interest in steam trains. News of an excursion worked by steam was guaranteed to draw people from a distance to

Youthful excitement pervades a photographic stop at Cole Green on the Hertford branch. (*H. C. Smith*)

Next stop was Hertingfordbury for another 'photo call'—Driver Fred Winter, meanwhile, 'takes the weight off'. (*H. C. Smith*)

witness our historic progress. Also I could not resist the thought that Kodak and its shareholders were poised for a bright future by the photographic interest we were creating. Apart from being a most pleasant excursion, it also presented us with our first opportunity to work a real passenger train, the first worked on BR by a privately preserved locomotive. It was an occasion which stands out among the many exploits 1247 and I were to share.

Railway preservation had by this time really begun to catch on, and I received a telephone call in my office from Alan Pegler. We had not met, but I knew of Alan through his connection with the Eastern Region Board. He told me that he was planning to acquire Gresley Class 'A3' 'Pacific' No 4472 *Flying Scotsman* and suggested that I might like to participate in it with him. I was, understandably, flattered by his invitation and very interested in such an exciting proposition. My mind flashed back to the 'temptations' during my visit to Top Shed with Colin Morris in 1959 when common sense and sound friendly advice had guided me toward the decision to acquire 'the Old Lady' which was, without doubt, the best engine for my purpose.

The vision of those splendid Gresley 'Pacifics' again loomed large and clear before my eyes. But I was not in the income bracket of Alan, and 4472 would be a heavy maintenance and operating commitment. Furthermore, I had ownership of 1247 to consider. It would have been impossible for me to become involved with two loco-motives, and disposal of the little Ivatt was out of the question. By this time, I had become deeply attached to 'the Old Lady'.

Obviously a straight negative to such a kind and exciting invitation was out of the question, and I asked Alan if I might have a day or so to ponder the idea. Understand-ably, the next three or four nights were pretty restless affairs, but eventually I telephoned Alan, declining his invitation on financial grounds and also because it would have involved giving up 1247. We had already been through and enjoyed too much together for that.

Subsequently, Alan teamed up with Cyril Palmer, an Eastern Region Motive Power Officer, and secured his locomotive. I was naturally intrigued by their project and, when Alan finally took over 4472, I went to King's Cross, met Colin Morris and together we stood at the end of Platform No 1 (adjacent to the site of the old East signal box) to watch the new owner proudly on the footplate for his engine's final BR journey to Doncaster.

4.
ARPS AND THE 'BLUE BELLE'

A TV series at that time, entitled *Railway Roundabout*, was proving an unqualified success. Produced with Children's Hour in mind, it was originally shown for children on Tuesday afternoons, but such was its popularity that a monthly showing on Thursday evenings for fathers had to be introduced to reduce the pressure on domestic TV sets on Tuesday afternoons! The series featured preserved locomotives and trains on both the standard and narrow gauge private lines which were emerging.

In connection with the series, I was invited by the BBC to their Birmingham Studio to take part in an interview by Peter Cranmer. Peter was an interesting and relaxed interviewer, and the whole affair was most enjoyable, exactly as one would have expected from hearing his informed and dignified cricket commentaries on radio.

The BBC also produced a short documentary entitled *The Most Exclusive Club in Britain* featuring the five private steam locomotive owners of that time and their engines: Lord Garnock (*The Great Marquess*), Brian Hollingsworth (LMS 'Black Five' No 5428, later *Bishop Eric Treacy*), Alan Pegler ('A3' 'Pacific' No 4472 *Flying Scotsman*), Pat Whitehouse (GWR 'Castle' Class No 7029 *Clun Castle*) and myself with No 1247.

A strong stirring of interest in railway preservation was now becoming felt and on 6 January 1962 a meeting was held in London to inaugurate the formation of the Railway Preservation Society, under the patronage of the Earl of Lanesborough. The founder members whose representatives were in attendance were the Bluebell Railway and the Middleton Railway Preservation Society. The aims of the RPS were presented to delegates who also attended, from the Festiniog Railway Society, the Industrial Locomotive Joint Preservation Committee, the Kent & East Sussex RPS, the Midland & Great Northern RPS, the South Devon Railway Society, the Talyllyn RPS, the West Highland Railway Society and the Consultative Panel for the Preservation of British Transport Relics.

Attention was called to the dependence of railway preservation schemes upon the voluntary support of enthusiasts, and the importance of co-operation between the various interested societies was stressed in order to avoid over-burdening this enthusiasm by a multiplicity of new projects which could easily jeopardise the position of existing ventures.

The Society would, it was hoped, be in a position to provide responsible expression of the combined experiences gained by existing societies in the field of railway preservation. It could, thereby, play an important role in presenting the case for railway preservation at large, in providing advice and information on new projects and in reconciling competitive schemes. I was honoured by an invitation to become the first Chairman of the Society, but the main driving force soon proved to be Captain Peter Manisty, Royal

Navy, at that time deeply involved in getting the Bluebell Railway 'out of the long grass'. I use these words because Peter kindly invited me to visit Sheffield Park in the early formative days to, as he put it, 'see what you think'. Whenever I hear music from *Oklahoma*, I recall the happy and exciting day we spent there, because as we pushed our way along the track between the platforms at Sheffield Park 'the grass was as high as an elephant's eye'. But what a transformation was quickly achieved there, and what a splendid and virile Bluebell Railway has emerged!

After a year or so, the RPS developed into the Association of Railway Preservation Societies, when Peter succeeded me as Chairman and steered it from strength to strength. The considerable and thriving 'private railway industry' in Britain today stems from the efforts and guidance of that organisation. In recognition of his magnificent and sustained efforts for over 20 years, Peter was deservedly awarded the MBE – but I am rushing on too quickly.

In the spring of 1961 contact was made by the Midland Section of the Stephenson Loco-motive Society who were planning a rail-tour from Birmingham (New Street) to traverse some Hertfordshire branch lines on Saturday 14 April. Their Mr W. A. Camwell wrote asking if 1247 could work the train whilst it was in GN territory. This was another 'Lea Flyer' type of job in which we would be taking over the train from the Midland at Hitchin and handing it back to them at Luton (Bute Street). The train was to be made up of six cars, which suited us well for working at passenger train speeds.

The Northampton–Bedford branch over which the excursion was to travel had lost its passenger service a week beforehand, while the Bedford–Hitchin section was 'freight only' and likely to be closed entirely at any time. The full itinerary was Birmingham

(New Street) to Nuneaton Abbey Street and Trent Valley, the Coventry avoiding line, Rugby, Northampton, Bedford, Hitchin, Hertford North, Welwyn Garden City, Hatfield, Luton, Dunstable, Leighton Buzzard, Weedon, Leamington Spa, Berkswell and Birmingham (New Street). In all, seven branch lines were to be traversed by the 'special'.

Motive power was provided by a Fowler '2P' from Birmingham (New Street) to Bedford, Class '2MT' (tank) Bedford to Hitchin, 1247 Hitchin to Luton via Hertford North and Hatfield, with the '2P' taking the train from us there and working it back to Birmingham.

On Saturday morning, we prepared and set off 'light' to Hitchin and, upon arrival, were crossed to the up side and put in the siding to the south of the station. We were kept there for a considerable time, but the 'special' eventually arrived, 100 minutes down. It was headed by a particularly dirty and untidy Midland Class '2MT' which was taken off and we set back on to the train in the up platform.

Setting off briskly on the up slow road, the driver put up a lively display to Stevenage and then through Langley Junction for a gallop to Watton-at-Stone and Hertford (North) where we made a booked stop for water. From Hertford we were routed over the 'freight only' line to Welwyn Garden City which we had earlier traversed with 'The Lea Flyer', and then on to Hatfield where we ran round and crossed the main line to the down side in readiness for returning north to the Luton and Dunstable Branch.

The crew that day were thoroughly enjoying themselves, and again we set off in fine style and fairly rattled along through Welwyn Garden City to Ayot where we were checked to cross with an up passenger train. Then to Wheathampstead, Harpenden (East) and so to Luton (Bute Street).

That branch line was not only picturesque, but ideal for a bit of sharp locomotive performance, particularly if the train was 'kept on the move'. We certainly

SATURDAY, 14th APRIL

1X47. RAIL TOUR
STEPHENSON LOCO. SOCIETY—BIRMINGHAM TO LUTON

Class						A
						p.m.
Hitchin	....	....	....	....	....	1 23
„	....	....	....	....	....	1 33
						8L
Langley Junction	....	....	....	....	1 49
Hertford North	....	....	....	....	2 12
„	....	....	....	....		2 22
Cole Green	....	....	....	....		2 32
						A
Welwyn Garden City	....	....	....	....	2 54
Hatfield	....	....	....	....		3 2
„	....	....	....	....		3 47
Ayot	....	....	....	....	....	4 1
„	....	....	....	...;	....	4F24
Harpenden East	....	....	....	....	4a40
Luton B. Street	....	....	....	...		4 56

A.—Time allowed for Train Crew to operate gates at Birchall and Attimore Level Crossings.
F.—Cross 2213 and 2555K.
STOCK.—B.S.O., 4 S.O., B.S.O.

Special Traffic Notice for our leg of the SLS rail tour.

showed off a bit that day for we were determined to knock something off the delay we had inherited at Hitchin. At Bute Street, we came off and the elegant Fowler '2P' took over. By dint of our crew keeping the train on the move and some very loose timing, the 'special' left for Birmingham on time, although I have no information as to what happened thereafter. One thing was certain, we had given the passengers fun for their money between Hitchin and Hertford and on the Luton branch.

For our part, we had enjoyed a particularly pleasant day out and, to round it all off, we cantered 'light' back along the branch to Welwyn Garden City and then south to Marshmoor, another great day behind us. 'The Old Lady' had put up a splendid show, and it could now be said that we had settled down with quiet confidence to fully enjoy these excursions in a completely relaxed way.

To mark the inauguration of the RPA, it was proposed that a special train would run from London to Sheffield Park, the Sussex headquarters of the Bluebell Railway, and to my surprise and delight it was suggested that 1247 should work the train – this was to be success indeed. The train working would involve not only Eastern Region but acceptance by all other regions since at some stage we would be traversing Midland, Western and, more extensively, Southern Region metals.

To my surprise, no objection was raised by the Midland and Western Regions, but the Southern, whose Brighton main line would be involved, was not at all happy. Of course, Southern Region was by that time an intensive 'electric tramway' operation, and they seemed disinclined to have anything to do with our 'Blue Belle' project.

The main sticking point was the Croydon office of the Central Division, and to 'free the wheels' an appointment was made for Peter Manisty and myself to call upon George Weedon, the Line Traffic Manager, in whose hands rested the power of veto and/or approval. We were not in the least interested in 'veto', but for a long time it seemed that was to be the only outcome. Mr Weedon was not in the least impressed, but by dint of some fast talking and frequent emphasis of 'the Old Lady's' impeccable record on Eastern Region, he at last gave approval – but not very happily.

He obviously had visions of a 63-year-old steam engine failing and blocking his prestigious Brighton electric service. We had other ideas, but from that day I knew that this was 'the big one'. If we fell down or stopped anything on the Southern, they would make such a stink that we would be barred henceforth from BR metals, everywhere.

Unfortunately, the original plan had to be abandoned because insufficient watering facilities remained to meet the locomotive's requirements with the train load envisaged.

A revised plan was prepared for working the train out of and back to Victoria, but it then transpired that at the time we wished to travel Southern Region were hampered by extensive engineering works in the Clapham and Streatham Junction areas, and any attempt to work us through the consequent congestion at our 25/30 mph would have further jeopardised their services.

To their credit, it must be said that George Weedon and his Southern Region colleagues worked whole-heartedly to find a solution, and it was ultimately agreed to work the train out of and back to London Bridge. We were not to be allowed to run 'light' in either direction by way of King's Cross, Holborn and Blackfriars, but were diagrammed by the longer route by way of Canonbury, Willesden, Old Oak Common and Crystal Palace. This meant two much longer trips on BR metals, so I was delighted. However, the movement outward on the Saturday had to be completed by mid-afternoon as engineering work on Saturday/Sunday night involved closure of both up and down lines between Latchmere and Clapham Junctions, making our presence the more sensitive.

Planning and re-planning went on day by day, but at last the anxiously awaited STN was issued. On 31 March 1962, the day prior to the 'Belle' working, we were diagrammed to travel 'light' up the main line to Finsbury Park, thence to Canonbury where we were to join the Broad Street line of the Midland, travelling on their metals to Willesden. At that point we were to be transferred to Western Region to take us round the west side of London through Old Oak Common, then over the Thames to Herne Hill, Crystal Palace and eventually round to Bricklayers Arms MPD where we were to be shedded overnight, ready to pick up the train at London Bridge on the following (Sunday) morning.

When the day came, we left Marshmoor in beautiful sunshine and set out for a unique journey round London. The diagram placed no pressure upon us, and we were able to drift along unfamiliar but exciting lines without coal or water problems. It was a memorable day, all went well and we reached Bricklayers Arms in the mid-afternoon to find Peter Manisty and his excited small daughter Jane waiting to greet us. Peter was always 'the enthusiast', and at the sight of the engine entering the shed he jumped in the air with joy (and, I suspect, no small measure of relief that we had safely accomplished Stage 1 of the exercise).

Readers who have visited a steam running shed a week or so before closure will appreciate the depressing sight that met our eyes. Bricklayers Arms at the time of our visit was in just that situation. As we drifted into the shed that afternoon, there was no visible sign of life. The only other occupants were three dirty, rusting and neglected Class '2MT' tanks, their appearance suggesting that one-way tickets to Barry had already been issued. A fresh breeze blew clouds of white dust everywhere from the endless heaps of ash which littered the neglected shed area. It was a depressing welcome, and Frank Knight suggested we 'dispose' as quickly as possible and get away home, returning at 4 am the next morning, as we were due off shed at 9.10 am for a 10.02 am

SATURDAY, 31st MARCH

LIGHT ENGINE

Class	G
	p.m.
Marshmoor	2‖A55
	8L
Potters Bar	3 6
Wood Green	3 26
Finsbury Park	3 33
Canonbury Junction	3*40
,,	3 44
Dalston East Junction	3 W50
,, ...	4L 0
Bricklayers Arms	5‖55

A.—J.52 Engine (privately owned).

Saturday, 31st March—continued

14—LIGHT ENGINE. (ex L.N.E.R. Class J.52—privately owned).

	p.m.			p.m.
Marshmoor (E.R.) ...	2 55		Latchmere Jn.	4/55
	—DN—		Clapham Jn. ... {	4W58
Canonbury ... {	3 40	§—Engine to stable and remain in steam over-		5 8LL
	3 44	night in readiness to work 10.2 a.m. London	Balham Jn.	5/15
Dalston Eastern Jn. {	3W50	Bridge to Sheffield Park, Sunday 1st April.	Streatham Hill ...	5/18
	4CM 0		Crystal Palace	5/26
Camden Road Jn. ...	4/11		Sydenham	5/33LL
Willesden H.L. Jn. ...	4/32		Forest Hill	5/36
Mitre Bridge Jn. ...	4a35 CM	(Bricklayers Arms (MPD) depart 9‖10 a.m. to	Bricklayers Arms Jn. ...	5/46
North Pole Jn. ...	4/37	London Bridge, via North Kent East Jn.,	Bricklayers A. M.P.D.	5 55§
Kensington (O) {	4CM46	Sunday 1st April).		
	4 47			

Special Traffic Notices for our light engine movement from Marshmoor to Bricklayers Arms, 31 March 1962.

London Bridge departure.

When I reached the shed the next morning, I spotted Frank's 'combination' parked inside the gates, and by the time I got to 1247 he was already busily coaling. It was a laborious and time-consuming operation – sacks had to be filled from the stack some distance away, carried to the engine and up a short, rickety ladder for tipping into the bunker. Whilst we concentrated on packing as much coal as possible into the bunker, a hose was topping up the saddle. We then embarked upon a thorough preparation of the engine, and Frank's energy and enthusiasm were boundless, as though his life depended upon it.

BBC cameras were to film the 'Blue Belle' to provide material for a new television series, so when preparation was completed we had to embark upon a thorough clean of the whole engine – our GN livery now wore a thick coating of grey BR ash. By the time a Brighton crew appeared to work the locomotive we were quite exhausted, but at least the engine was ready and had recovered her visual identity, ready to appear before a critical public. So at 9.10 am we set off at a leisurely pace for London Bridge where a six-car Southern set – and lots of people – awaited us.

The platform was thronged with many of

Ready for the off—1247 stands at London Bridge with the 'Blue Belle', 1 April 1962.

the 400 booked passengers, but the festive spirit did not spread to the footplate, where the 'approaching retirement' Brighton driver was a far from happy man. He was naturally unfamiliar with the engine and unaware of her capabilities. But he was aware, and painfully so, that he would be working among 'the Brightons' and that water availability on our route was such that not a drop must be wasted. However, Frank bolstered his confidence at every opportunity. I knew that no GN engine was going to get into trouble whilst Frank was at hand, but unfortunately the Brighton driver did not have that knowledge until very much later that day!

It is perhaps appropriate at this stage to touch briefly upon the origin of some of the lines traversed by the 'Blue Belle' that day. The first section covered by this unique and historic 'special' was mainly on arches as far as Corbetts Lane (1³/4 miles) and formed part of the London & Greenwich Railway opened in 1836. The next 7³/4 miles to the Jolly Sailor (Norwood) formed part of the London & Croydon Railway, famous for its experimental atmospheric system. Opened in June 1839, it continued through to the present West Croydon. Then followed 5 miles of London & Brighton track to Stoats Nest (Coulsdon) serving the not-very-adjacent Epsom Racecourse. The next 6¹/2 miles to Earlswood Common were the South Eastern's, friction over which led to the LB & SCR eventually building in 1900 the alternative Quarry line avoiding Redhill and over which we were routed. From Earlswood to Haywards Heath was 'Brighton' territory, opened in July 1841. The route included tunnels at Merstham (1,831 yards) and Balcombe (1,141 yards) and Rastrick's 37-arch Ouse Viaduct which rises to a height of 100 feet above ground. In all it is quite an exacting route, with long 1 in 264 gradients in either direction.

We left London Bridge promptly at 10.02 am and made booked stops at Norwood Junction for water, East Croydon for passengers, and Three Bridges for water and to allow Dr Beeching, Chairman of British Railways, and Mrs Beeching to join the train.

Dr Beeching came on to the footplate,

En route—crossing the splendid Ouse Viaduct, and taking the Ardingley branch at Copyhold Junction with steam to spare. (*R. C. Riley*)

Sunday, 1st April

Engine No.	ER.J.52 Class		Engine No.	ER.J.52 Class
After working ...	Depot		After working ...	3.35 p.m. Sheffield Park
	a.m.			p.m.
Bricklayers Arms M.P.D.	9 10			
North Kent East Jn. ...	9e23		London Bridge (Ctl.) ...	7 25
London Bridge (Ctl.) ...	9 30		North Kent East Jn. ...	7e35
			Bricklayers Arms M.P.D.	7 45
To work	10.2 a.m. Sheffield Park		To work	Depot

Speed **not** to exceed 25 m.p.h.   Speed **not** to exceed 25 m.p.h.

Sunday, 1st April—continued

25—LONDON BRIDGE, EAST CROYDON, HORSTED KEYNES AND SHEFFIELD PARK.
Excursion to Bluebell Railway.

	a.m.			p.m.
London Bridge (No. 16 Platform) ...	10 2LL	Formation: BSO	Sheffield Park (Bluebell Line)	3 35
Bricklayers Arms Jn. ...	10/ 9LL	4 SO		3 50
Forest Hill	10/19	BSO.	Horsted Keynes	
Norwood Jn.	10/28LL			4 26
Windmill Bridge Jn. ...	10/32LL	Train hauled by ex E.Region J.52 class loco-	Copyhold Jn. ...	4/36
East Croydon ...	10§34W	motive No. 1247.		4 40RR
	10 39LL		Haywards Heath	
Coulsdon North... ...	10/52QL	§—Train calls to pick up/set down passengers,		4 54
Earlswood ...	11/12LL	in addition to engine taking water.	Three Bridges ...	5W18LL
Three Bridges ...	11§32W			5§28
	11 36	**ROUTE RESTRICTION.**	Earlswood ...	5/50QL
Copyhold Jn. ...	11/55LL	Train must run via Quarry Line in each	Coulsdon North ...	6/11LL
	12 0RR	direction.	East Croydon ...	6§23W
Haywards Heath				6 28
	12 17		Windmill Bridge Jn. ...	6/31LL
Copyhold Jn. ...	12/21	**HORSTED KEYNES**	Norwood Jn. ...	6/36TL
	12 30	The Local special instructions to Signalmen	Forest Hill	6/45
Horsted Keynes		at Horsted Keynes and also to Hand Signalmen,	Bricklayers Arms Jn. ...	6/55TL
	12 40	Shunters and Motive Power Conductors must be	London Bridge	
Sheffield Park (Bluebell Line) ...	1 5	observed when the special train travels to and returns from the Bluebell Railway.	(No. 15 Platform) ...	7 0

Special Traffic Notice for the 'Blue Belle', 1 April 1962.

spoke to the crew and was 'pictured' in various poses by a battery of photographers of the local and national Press. These frivolities over, we set off for Haywards Heath where we ran round the train and set off, bunker first, through Copyhold Junction to Ardingly and Horsted Keynes.

At a Press Conference in the guard's compartment, Dr Beeching was quoted as saying, 'I'm interested in railway preservation in its right place. This is an excellent example of it'. I was told that he did not comment on the suggestion that the Bluebell Railway acquired its name from passengers who, in BR days, were kept so

long waiting at stations that they had time to pick bluebells. These days there can surely be few more pleasant and interesting places to do so. From what I saw of Dr Beeching that day, he was a very pleasant man who thoroughly entered into the spirit of the occasion with the obvious intention of enjoying the day's proceedings.

Upon arrival at Horsted Keynes, the Southern crew left the engine to await our return there, and we then had the footplate to ourselves. A Stroudley 'Terrier', *Stepney*, was attached to the south end of the train whilst we remained attached to the rear. The 'Terrier' experienced some difficulty in

Arriving at Horsted Keynes on the Bluebell Railway. (*R. C. Riley*)

Stroudley 'Terrier' No 55 *Stepney* was attached to the other end of the stock to draw us down the preserved line.

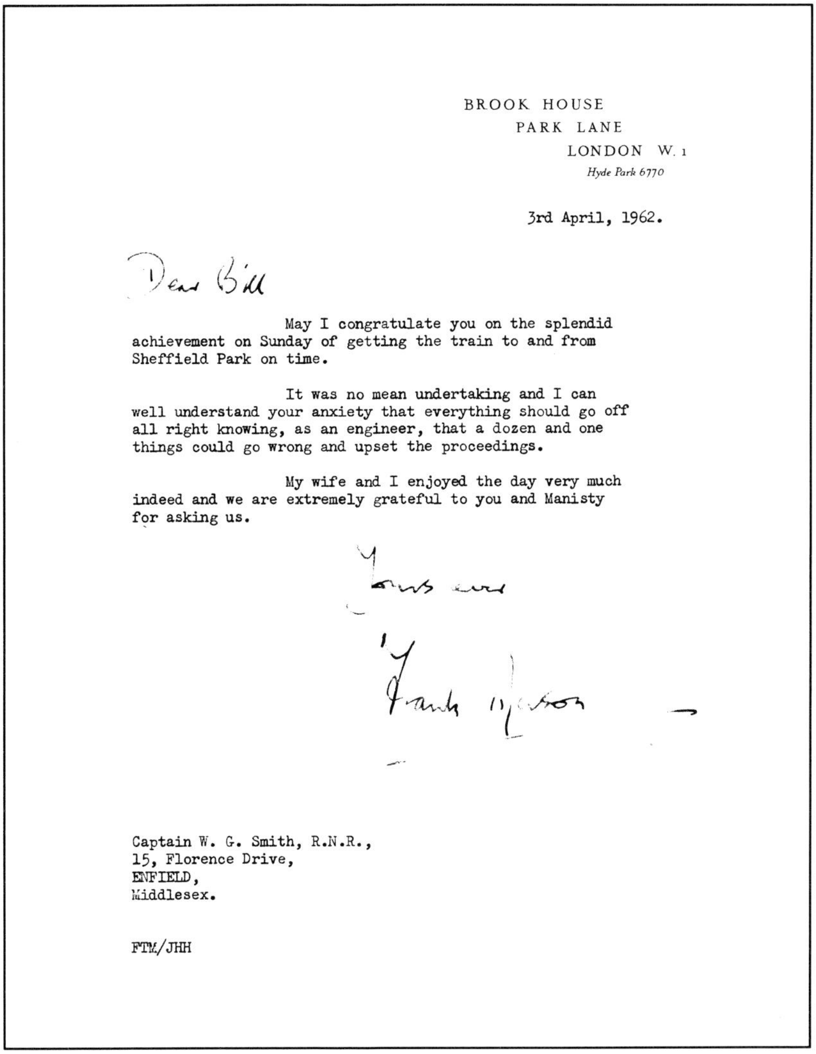

BROOK HOUSE
PARK LANE
LONDON W. 1
Hyde Park 6770

3rd April, 1962.

Dear Bill

　　　　May I congratulate you on the splendid achievement on Sunday of getting the train to and from Sheffield Park on time.

　　　　It was no mean undertaking and I can well understand your anxiety that everything should go off all right knowing, as an engineer, that a dozen and one things could go wrong and upset the proceedings.

　　　　My wife and I enjoyed the day very much indeed and we are extremely grateful to you and Manisty for asking us.

Yours ever

Frank Mason

Captain W. G. Smith, R.N.R.,
15, Florence Drive,
ENFIELD,
Middlesex.

FTM/JHH

A treasured note from Vice Admiral Sir Frank Mason KCB, Engineer-in-Chief of the Fleet 1953-57.

moving the train, plus 1247, through the curve out of the station, and I was obliged – quite contrary to the regulations in force there – to 'give a little support' with the aid of which the train moved on to the final stage of its journey to Sheffield Park and a tumultuous welcome. The train stopped briefly at a new Bluebell Station named Holywell (Waterworks) which Dr Beeching 'opened'.

Also guests on that day were Vice Admiral Sir Frank and Lady Mason. A year

or so previously Admiral Mason had retired from the appointment of Engineer in Chief of the Fleet, leaving behind him a life-long record of outstanding engineering achievement in the Royal Navy.

The enthusiastic and warm welcome did not obscure my view of the great transformation which had been achieved at Sheffield Park since my first visit with Peter Manisty some years earlier. After the passengers had alighted, the 'Terrier' moved the train forward to release us so that we

Ready to return to London Bridge, 1247 stands at the head of the train at Horsted Keynes. (R. C. *Riley*)

Last lap—the 'Blue Belle' passes Star Lane, Coulsdon, on the return journey to London Bridge. (R.C. *Riley*)

could cross over to the coal dock, where willing and energetic Bluebell volunteers replenished our depleted bunker and topped up the saddle.

After a welcome wash and a most enjoyable lunch in a nearby buffet car, we rejoined 1247 and moved across to the up platform where we were re-attached. Our journey back along the Bluebell Railway was most enjoyable, providing me with my first opportunity to drive 1247 when working a loaded passenger train. At Horsted Keynes we ran round the train and the Southern crew rejoined us, looking no less unhappy. To the accompaniment of enthusiastic cheering, we departed Horsted Keynes, 2 minutes down, and passed through Copy-hold Junction on to the Brighton main line. At Haywards Heath we ran round the train once more and were ready for a bunker-first return to London Bridge.

We had filled the saddle to capacity at Sheffield Park, after which our next booked stops for water were Three Bridges and East Croydon. This thought must have been playing on the mind of our driver since it was reflected in his face. We set off 4 minutes down and had a good run, the locomotive making a brave showing on the gradients we encountered. But we had not cleared Balcombe Tunnel before the driver was chuntering about 'no water' and wanting to shut off. He obviously had little experience of small tank engines, but Frank smoothed him down, pointing out that although the water was only just above the bottom nut of the gauge glass, we were running bunker-first uphill, and that all would be well when we hit level – 'Just keep her going,' he said. And so it was, for once we got on the level, water came back into the gauge – but not far! Frank cosseted and encouraged the driver all the way to Three Bridges, by which time, I must admit, I was feeling some concern myself. Then on to East Croydon and more water. Whilst we were under the water column, the 'Brighton Belle', having been following us, thundered through on the fast road, stressing how vital it was to keep time on routes such as that, or

for that matter on all BR lines upon which we were allowed to work.

The run up to London Bridge was very pleasant in the evening sunshine and, encountering no checks, we ran in 5 minutes before time. 'The Old Lady' was naturally a centre of admiration for our passengers and the travelling public alike whilst we were 'trapped in' by the stock.

The driver relaxed a little and at one point I detected a weak smile – what a pity that a glorious fun day for so many proved to be such a stressful burden for him! I could only hope that he had volunteered for the job – at least it would then give him a nice warm feeling when he reached home, and his slippers.

For us it was another night at Bricklayers Arms, but with not such an early start on Monday morning, since no one wanted to be bothered with us until the morning peak was disposed of. We left, as booked, at 11.40 am for a pleasant return run 'light' to retrace our fascinating circular route of the capital to Finsbury Park and on to Marshmoor before the evening peak. That Monday journey was a delight – we had no pressures and the previous day's important job was safely behind us. And we had plenty of water!

It would be most improper and unfair were

MONDAY, 2nd APRIL

ADDITIONAL LIGHT ENGINE

Class						G
Bricklayers Arms M.P.D.	....	....	....		....	a.m. 11 ‖A40
Dalston East Junction		....	....		....	p.m. 1 W45
			....	....	....	1 L55
Dalston West Junction	"	....		....	....	1X56
Canonbury Junction	....	....		....	....	2ₐ 0
		....	....	....	....	2 8
Finsbury Park	....	"	....	....	....	2 15
						8L
Wood Green	...ᵣ	....	....	....	....	2 24
Potters Bar	....	....	....	....	....	2 44
Marshmoor	....	....	....	....	....	2 ‖55

Our return journey from Bricklayers Arms.

I not at this point to pay tribute to the exemplary role of Frank Knight in the 'Blue Belle' operation. It could not have succeeded, let alone been the outstanding success that it was, without his skill, quiet determination and sheer hard work on those three memorable days. His was a contribution, unseen by the majority, but a vital ingredient throughout.

On the lighter side, rumour had it that George Weedon had taken the precaution of stationing 'pilots' at strategic points *en route* to recover and/or assist had we got into trouble whilst in his territory on the Sunday. I certainly saw no sign of any such 'pilots', so perhaps it was all a leg-pull or a ruse to keep us on our toes. That was never necessary – we were always on our toes and, in the proper hands, that 'J52' can move mountains!

As so often happens in this life, the upsets come along hot on the heels of periods of calm and stability, and so it was with 1247

and our main-line exploits.

I cannot recall precisely how we were informed, but informed we were, that all steam excursions were at an end, and no more were we to be allowed to work on BR tracks. We were not singled out in this matter, and other privately owned locomotives, with the exception of No 4472 *Flying Scotsman*, were all similarly 'warned off'. Fortunately Alan Pegler had secured the running future of his locomotive by means of a legal agreement with BR.

This obviously called for an entirely new think insofar as future locomotive working was concerned, but at least 1247 had achieved the distinction of being the first privately owned steam locomotive to work passenger trains over BR metals, and we had enjoyed a very good run for our money from July 1959 until April 1962.

Observing the mad scramble by BR over recent years to obtain National Railway Museum and Steam Locomotive Operators Association steam locomotives to work their prestigious tourist trains, I cannot but recall the unceremonious manner in which we were asked to leave almost 30 years previously.

5.
TO YORKSHIRE

Through the kindness of Dr John Coiley, the Keeper of the National Railway Museum at York, I was privileged to be included in the crew which accompanied his replica of Stephenson's *Rocket* when it was first exhibited in Kensington Gardens and, subsequently, when she visited Sacramento, Osaka and Vancouver. These were delightful affairs through which I made many friends from among the crew members and enthusiasts domiciled in the countries we visited.

It was with surprise and great pleasure that in the summer of 1985 I received an invitation to drive *Rocket* for three days during the celebrations to mark the 10th Anniversary of the opening of the National Railway Museum. My co-driver was a close railway friend and Doncaster Works apprentice (1940), Peter Coxon, and with a highly compatible sense of humour the promise of a memorable and enjoyable weekend was fully justified. Peter had been a *Rocket* crew member when the replica first appeared in steam in Kensington Gardens, and is a rostered driver on the Leighton Buzzard Narrow Gauge Railway.

On the first day, *Rocket* was at her temperamental worst, and we were hard pressed to put on a good show, running up and down in the yard whilst Dame Margaret Weston, the Director of the Science Museum, Dr Coiley, their distinguished guests and local dignitaries were in evidence. We were almost reduced to pushing the

locomotive, but we got away with it, and on the two following days *Rocket* atoned and ran like a bird!

Our instructions on the matter of footplate rides were quite explicit – no access to the footplate, or rides, without a signed permit. There did not seem to be many permits about, but on the Saturday (the second day of the proceedings) a smartly dressed young man approached the engine and presented his signed 'permit to ride'. He was welcomed to the footplate, and we proceeded to entertain him. It was difficult to accurately assess his age as he wore a heavy but neatly trimmed beard, but I placed him as being in the region of 40.

He enjoyed his ride and as we bade him farewell and he commenced to dismount from the footplate, he turned and surprised me by saying, 'It's a long time since I last saw you'. I had to apologise and confess that I could not recall our previous meeting. He then explained that, as a small boy, he spent much of his time watching the trains at his local station. One Sunday afternoon, just as he had thoughts of setting off home for his tea, the signal to the platform upon which he was standing came 'off' and he decided to wait to see what was coming. His patience was rewarded when, to his amazement, he saw a bright green 'steamer' approaching which then stopped right beside him and proceeded to take water.

He went on to say, 'It was one of the most exciting moments of my life. I remember it all so clearly – it was the "Blue Belle" at East Croydon. We didn't get many steamers there in those days.' How I wish Geoffrey Huskisson and Colin Morris could have heard his words. It was precisely with thoughts for the small boys of the future that in early 1959 I had told them of my wish to preserve a steam locomotive.

Although enthusiasm for preserved steam continued to increase steadily following the subsequent relaxing of BR's attitude, few seemed inclined to contribute towards it by buying a ticket. Whilst thousands would flock to the lineside and hang with cameras poised from every conceivable vantage point, we often failed to fill the stock with fare-paying passengers. To the frustration of BR and ourselves, cancellations were a regular occurrence and nothing could be taken as a certainty until we were actually coupled up at the departure point.

It is a situation which, I understand, persists today, but circumstances are somewhat different. In those early days enthusiast 'specials' operated only every three or four months and were confined to the North London/Herts area where 1247 was the only privately restored locomotive available.

Today steam excursions operate countrywide on an almost weekly basis. But I do not believe market saturation is the only problem. The main stumbling block is the demand of 'gricers' for no-cost photographic opportunities. They seek the photographic reward for which others are expected to pay the bill. How unfortunate that the benefiting film manufacturers cannot be encouraged to emulate the generous financial and practical support given by British Coal.

As Chairman of the Railway Preservation Society, I arranged to visit the Middleton Railway in Leeds on Saturday 19 May 1962, and was shown round by Dr Fred Youell, the Chairman, who kindly offered me a bed for the night in his home to enable me more conveniently to push on the next day to the newly formed Keighley & Worth Valley Railway.

On the following morning I was collected by John Bellwood, Vice Chairman of that railway, and taken to Howarth to meet Bob Cryer their Chairman, Hubert Foster, Ralph Povey, Secretary Tony Cox and their colleagues to see the progress they were making towards opening the line. It ran from Oxenhope, through Howarth, Oakworth, and Ingrow, down to Keighley where they were to enjoy the advantage of using station platforms adjacent to and connected with those served by BR.

The line was ideal for operating as a private railway and I was impressed by its potential and the people who were involved in its development – they were an active and enthusiastic group. With only two 0-4-0 industrial locomotives available to them, I was asked if there was any possibility of 1247 being sent to Howarth. At that time I was in the course of severing connection with my employers at Marshmoor, and moving to join my brother in a manufacturing group which, although an appreciable rail-freight customer, did not have a private siding or steam shed similar to that which had accommodated 1247 at Marshmoor, but in which she could not be housed in future. Additionally, as I have already mentioned, privately owned locomotives, with the exception of *Flying Scotsman*, could no longer work on BR tracks.

There was accordingly no reason why 1247 should not go to Howarth to support and help set up what had all the makings of becoming a highly successful private railway undertaking. Approval was given by BR to run 'light' from Marshmoor to Keighley by night, and we were booked to leave in the late afternoon of 4 March 1965, making a short day stop-over at New England MPD, then continuing the next night and reaching Keighley on the morning of 6 March.

It was with very mixed feelings that we set off from Marshmoor, and excitement was not one of them. Were we not leaving a shed full of happy memories and the scene of so many achievements, the friendly and helpful King's Cross District of BR which had supported and trusted us from the start to keep out of trouble, and all our friendly and familiar Hertfordshire branch lines? Frank was with us as usual, but I could not help thinking that this must surely be our last trip together, and that was not a heart-warming thought either.

Sadly, moving from Marshmoor also meant leaving behind two other old and hard-working friends, *Shirley* and *London John*. One of my last tasks was to obtain quotations for and then place on order a six-wheeled diesel locomotive to take over the shunting of the Works sidings. No doubt in the fullness of time the diesel was delivered and put into service. I have often wondered what happened to those two immaculate and well-maintained 'steamers', but sadly I have never been able to ascertain details of their disposal.

I sincerely hope they were not 'put to the torch'. They had many years of useful service left when last I saw them and could have been a great help to many of the smaller private railways then slowly emerging from their chrysalis.

Our pleasant run to New England followed its customary relaxed pattern, and sliding slowly into the shed there, we were greeted by the rotund and smiling figure of Mr Wooffenden, the Shedmaster. Conversion of his Depot to diesel traction was by that time complete, but he had cleared a quiet corner for us and a continuous guard was mounted to ensure that vandals were kept at bay. He was particularly friendly and invited me into his Store where he had looked out a number of small items of obsolete 'J52' parts in readiness for our visit. As he remarked, 'They will be more use in your tool-box than in my scrap bin!'. It was a very kind and thoughtful gesture and he certainly took great care of 'the Old Lady' until we returned the following evening to continue on our way.

The route to Keighley took us through Grantham and Newark to Doncaster, where we left the East Coast Main Line for Wakefield, Bramley, Bradford, Shipley and Bingley. It was an interesting trip, even in the dark, and we were safely in the old carriage sidings at Keighley by breakfast time next morning. Although the Keighley & Worth Valley Railway had been founded in March 1962, it was not until June 1968 that all formalities and granting of their Light Railway Order were completed. However, BR were very helpful and, from February 1965, allowed them to stable various items in the Keighley carriage sidings where they were assembled when we arrived. The arrival of 1247 in steam, and further co-operation by BR, provided an opportunity for the K & WVR to get the accumulated items up the branch and safely to Howarth yard.

Firstly, we attached Gresley Class 'N2' No 4744 and a GNR bogie milk-van to form the first train up the branch. This surely must have been the patiently awaited re-birth of that railway, and excitement ran high. The weather was overcast and bitterly cold, with a sprinkling of snow and very hard frost. When passing through the long-unused tunnels, the blast from the engine brought down heavy falls of caked soot and a cascade of large icicles which crashed upon the engine cab and vehicle roofs like rifle fire.

Having placed our first train in Howarth yard, we returned 'light' to Keighley carriage sidings where we attached L&Y locomotive No 957, a SE&CR matchboard brake and a MS&LR four-wheeler, and again proceeded with them up the branch to Howarth.

Leaving 'the Old Lady' so far from home in Howarth yard was not a very heart-warming occasion, but John Bellwood, whose current home was nearby, undertook to keep an eye on her and ensure that she was only steamed if he or I could be present to prepare her.

Establishing a safe, reliable private railway out of a semi-derelict, long-unused line, by the use of voluntary labour, is a costly, painstaking and lengthy business, and the K&WVR was no exception. Finality with BR not yet having been achieved, storage facilities were very limited and it was not an ideal situation for the 'J52' which was steamed only rarely during her stay. It is a pity that she was not still on the line when it re-opened in 1968, for she would have been

1247 hauls the first train up the Keighley & Worth Valley Railway, passing Ingrow in bitter weather on 6 March 1965. In tow are a milk-van and 'N2' No 4744 which, by July, was in steam and hauling trains itself (below). (*Anthony Cox, W. Hubert Foster*)

The following year, 1247 is seen in the hands of Driver John Bellwood on a permanent way train engaged in line clearance. At the time the drop-side wagon in the train was the only one of the type available to the K&WVR. (*W. Hubert Foster*)

1247 at Haworth station in 1966. (*W. Hubert Foster*)

an ideal locomotive to work on the splendid railway which then emerged and has over the years been developed and operated so successfully.

It was, of course, disappointing that 1247 saw so little work during her long stay at Howarth, and I was naturally concerned that this idleness with little or no shelter from the weather would be causing deterioration of the boiler and tubes.

I suspect that word of the locomotive's inactivity filtered through to Pat Whitehouse in Birmingham. We had not met, but he wrote asking if 1247 could go on loan to Tyseley. It was there that he kept his two locomotives, GWR 'Castle' Class No 7029 *Clun Castle* and LMS 'Jubilee' Class 4-6-0 No 5593 *Kolhapur*. In his letter he said that he envisaged running a steam service at weekends from Tyseley to Stratford-on-Avon which I naturally believed would put 'the Old Lady' back again into passenger working.

Transfer of 1247 from Howarth created no problem for the Keighley & Worth Valley as they were not yet ready to commence operations, and I accordingly agreed to the request. I learned later that a similar request for loan of his 'Black Five' No 5428 *Bishop Eric Treacy* had been made to Brian Hollingsworth. Application was duly made to BR for approval to run 'light' on their tracks to Tyseley, and this was granted in a very short space of time.

And so we were on our way again, but unfortunately not acc-ompanied by Frank Knight. The first step, a short one, was only as far as Holbeck MPD, where we made a night stop-over. The Midland Region had stipulated that, 'in light steam', we were to be hauled from that point to Tyseley by a diesel locomotive. Our brief stay at Holbeck provided an opportunity to meet up with Shedmaster Tommy Greaves, to whom 1247 had been well known at Hornsey MPD

before she was transferred to Top Shed.

If my memory serves me correctly, it was a Class '24' diesel which buffered up to us the next morning, and accompanied on the footplate by a 'conductor' for company, we set off on a rather undignified but interesting trip to Tyseley. I seem to recall that No 5428 *Bishop Eric Treacy* had arrived before us and we were placed up against her, in the open.

With hindsight, I believe an inspection beforehand by both Brian Hollingsworth and myself to ascertain what storage facilities were available would have been wise. Both engines were left in the open, and whilst the workshop personnel were excellent and their facilities good, they were at the time fully occupied in caring for their own locomotives. Covered accommodation was only sufficient to house the 'Castle' and the 'Jubilee', and it is unfortunate but true to say that 5428 and 1247 had of necessity to claim a low priority for attention. So far as steaming opportunities were concerned, I do not recall the 'J52' getting to Stratford on more than one occasion during her considerable stay. Since those early days progress and development at Tyseley, as I saw for myself quite recently, has been very considerable.

In October 1974, I received a telephone call from John Bellwood, who was at that time BR Traction Engineer (Running) at Newcastle. I had not heard from him since we were at Haworth together, and he told me that in his leisure time he was acting in the capacity of Hon General Manager of the North Yorkshire Moors Railway which was shortly planning to commence operating steam-hauled passenger trains from Grosmont, where they had a 'live' junction with the Esk Valley line of BR, to Pickering.

In common with all private railways in their formative years, motive power was at a premium and John was hard pressed. The question he posed was whether I would let 'the Old Lady' go to North Yorkshire, to which I replied that I had no objection. I said that although 1247 was not working at Tyseley, I would, in fairness to Pat Whitehouse, have to write showing him the

Tyseley days. 1247 'Black Five' No 5428 *Bishop Eric Treacy* on shed, and the pair separated by 'Castle' No 7029 *Clun Castle* at Stratford-upon-Avon in May 1970. (*R. C. Riley*)

courtesy of three months' notice. To my surprise, John explained that they would like the engine to move in a few days in company with *Bishop Eric Treacy*, No 5428, which was also moving from Tyseley to Grosmont, and the two could travel in company, at no extra cost. He suggested that to save time I could telephone Pat Whitehouse asking him to release my engine, and this I agreed to do. Pat was understandably not particularly amused, but agreed to release 1247, and I called John back to tell him he was in luck!

Preparation of the two locomotives for the considerable journey, and after such lengthy inactivity, was no light task and was undertaken by volunteers from Grosmont who travelled to Tyseley for that purpose. They were Chris Cubitt, a BR driver now based at Scarborough MPD, Maurice Burns, Mick Dewing, John Hunt, Peter Hutchinson and John Whitbread. After both loco-motives had been prepared, they were hauled by a diesel to Darlington and, by way of the Esk Valley line, to Grosmont. They left Tyseley on 3 November 1974 and

reached Grosmont on the 5th of that month. That was the only journey on BR track upon which I did not accompany 'the Old Lady', but she and 'the Bishop' could not have been in better hands, and both reached their destination mechanically sound, albeit in need of a thorough clean.

With the arrival of 1247 at Grosmont shed, operation, maintenance and repair of the locomotive was the responsibility of the Shedmaster, and at no time whilst the engine was on loan to the North York Moors Railway had I the slightest cause for comp-laint. In the early years, steam was restricted to the Grosmont–Goathland section, with the Pickering–Goathland section being served by a four-car Gloucester DMU set. We were originally denied use of Pickering station, and the south end of the line terminated at a halt at High Mill some 400 yards to the north of the station, where DMUs could reverse, but loco-hauled trains were unable to run-round.

In early 1975 we were granted permission to run into Pickering station, and the first passenger train to use the station was the

'The Old Lady' on the North Yorks Moors Railway: seen in August 1975 leaving Grosmont with a train to Goathland, in May 1978 with 'The North Yorkshireman' at Newtondale, and entering Pickering that same month with 'The North Eastern'. (*R. C. Riley*)

10.20 departure for Grosmont on Saturday 24 May of that year. The diagrammed train was a four-car Gloucester set which I had the pleasure of driving on that occasion. From that point on, with the station layout then available to us, we were able to work steam trains throughout the line from Grosmont to Pickering. It was at this point that 1247 became the oldest standard gauge steam locomotive to work timetabled passenger trains.

I received a letter in 1974 from a NYMR member working for Shell in Santo Domingo, directing my attention to a stamp printed by the Dominican Republic to mark their Centenary and depicting 1247 hauling the 'Blue Belle'. He was kind enough shortly afterwards to send me a good supply of stamps which were sold to collectors in support of NYMR funds. 1247 then became the first privately owned British locomotive to appear on a postage stamp, although Stanley Gibbons advise that English trains have frequently been depicted on foreign stamps.

'The Old Lady' steamed freely, but the odd driver failed to grasp that fact and sought salvation in a boiler full of water and a firebox full of coal – a sure recipe for disaster! I recall an occasion when I was in the up platform at Levisham with the four-car Gloucester DMU waiting to cross with 1247 coming from Pickering with a six-car train. When at last she appeared round the Farworth curve, it was obvious from her slow progress down the Levisham straight that she was in trouble – and the clouds of jet black smoke gave a clue as to the root of that trouble. As the 'J52' ran into the platform it was clear that, as I had suspected, she was

very short of steam and I could only hope that she had sufficient to operate the ejector. I believed and hoped that the driver would ask the guard for 2 minutes to find some steam, before setting off to climb through Newtondale to Goathland Summit, but to my dismay the train halted only briefly, then slowly set off again with belching clouds of black smoke filling the valley. News of the train's 'sticking' on the 1 in 49 gradient at Newton-dale reached Pickering shortly after we did, but thankfully there were few instances such as this during the six years the locomotive was shedded at Grosmont.

In each of three consecutive years, 1247 covered the highest annual locomotive mileage on the Moors, being economical to steam in both low and peak seasons. The summer trains at that time were not as heavy as those which have been worked in recent years, and the engine was therefore suitable for providing season-long support. Attention to running and brake gear (including wheel turning) and re-tubing was provided during winter non-running periods, and this work was the first required by the locomotive since being 'shopped' by BR in 1958.

In 1977, shortly after the completion of this mechanical work, 'the Old Lady' was involved in an unfortunate derailment which could have had very serious consequences. In the course of shunting operations on the shed at Grosmont, it was necessary to place one of the 'Black Fives' – No 4767 *George Stephenson* I believe – and 1247 on the shed road inside the south end of the Grosmont tunnel. The movement was carried out using a Drewry diesel shunter which was left coupled to the two 'cold' steamers.

Myself enjoying life on the NYMR! (*by courtesy of the Yorkshire Post*)

As invariably happens when laid-down safety procedures are not carried out, disaster struck. In this instance, the driver of the shunter brought the 'string' to rest by use of the direct air brake, left the engine running and abandoned the footplate. Unfortunately, before doing so he failed to apply the handbrake on the shunter, or on any of the steam locomotives attached. Shortly afterwards, a 'helpful' colleague chanced along and shut down the engine of the shunter. He failed to check that the handbrake was applied, and after an interval the air brake on the shunter became ineffective. The three locomotives moved off down the falling gradient, through the tunnel and towards Grosmont level crossing and station, which are protected by a set of 'traps' some 20 yards outside the north-end tunnel mouth.

Such was the speed and combined weight of the locomotives that when the leading locomotive, 1247, was derailed at the 'traps', the procession continued along the formation towards the parapet of the bridge over the River Esk, passage through the ballast ultimately bringing the 'string' to rest. 1247 sustained the damage, but fortunately the parapet of the bridge was not reached, which would have incurred far more serious consequences. Fortunately also, the locomotive came to rest before the front end of the 'Black Five' was derailed.

With a speed which would have done BR credit, the locomotives were recovered and very shortly thereafter Les Barwick, that maestro of the NYMR permanent way, and his men remedied the damage to the shed road and 'traps'. The mishap was ill-timed so far as 1247 was concerned. The newly completed brake renewals were wasted, since damage sustained through the derailment called for three new brake stretchers, some brake hangers, and repair of the brake weigh-shaft, a life-guard and the trailing spring hangers. However, the consequences could have been far more serious. Invaluable repair assistance was provided by BR Shildon Works, but 1247 did not re-enter service for some weeks.

On Saturday 5 May 1979, the NYMR Railway celebrated the 20th Anniversary of 1247 passing into private ownership by giving a lunch party in the GWR Saloon. Guests included Geoffrey Huskisson, D. W. (Bill) Harvey, Colin Morris, Peter Townend, John Bellwood and Michael L. Harris, who was at one time on the staff of Gerry Fiennes at Great Northern House. Also present was that well-known author of many railway works, Ossie Nock, who was invited by the Stephenson Locomotive Society, at that time celebrating their 70th Anniversary. The service train to which the Saloon was attached was worked from Grosmont to Pickering by 1247, after which lunch was served.

The Luncheon Party celebrating 20 years of private ownership of 1247, 5 May 1979. On the left, from the front, are Peter Townend, myself, Geoffrey Huskisson and Colin Morris; on the right, from the front, are B. Warr, John Bellwood, John Slater, editor of *The Railway Magazine*, and Michael Harris; O.S. Nock sits at the head of the table. We are seated in the GWR Saloon in Pickering station after having been attached to a service train from Grosmont, worked by 1247.

Lunch was a hilarious, light-hearted affair with much good-natured bantering. Bill Harvey revealed a special affection for 1247 which he recalled was Station Pilot at Doncaster in 1924 when he commenced his apprenticeship at the 'Plant'. He said that at that time she was 'still wearing her wartime battleship grey livery, lettered GNR and numbered 1247 in white characters'.

It transpired that a week or so prior to the luncheon Bill had dropped in at Grosmont to find the 'J52' on shed. After a few words with the Shedmaster he had removed his jacket, donned his dust-coat and proceeded to reset the locomotive's valves. A copy of his typical and carefully preserved notes came into my hands only recently, recording, as they do, his re-setting of the valves on 3 April 1979 and his diary entry for the birthday party on 5 May of that year.

It will be seen that the footnote to his diary entry records the attempt by dry-humoured Colin Morris to 'wind him up'. Colin complained that on the journey from Grosmont to Pickering incorrect valve settings were causing the locomotive to

'surge'. The Line Manager's Saloon in which we were travelling was attached to the rear of the train and, upon arrival at Pickering, Bill carried out an inspection which revealed that it was a loose coupling between the rear train-coach and the Saloon which was responsible for the surging. His face when returning to the Saloon was a picture of delight, and to the amusement of all present he revealed his findings. No surging was experienced on the return journey, during which the Saloon was immediately behind the engine!

Bill's visits to the shed never failed to bring a bonus in the form of the guidance and practical help he so generously and enthusiastically provided. He is without doubt the finest practical steam locomotive engineer of his generation. He possesses those great gifts of patience and thoroughness, and honesty and integrity are personified in everything he undertakes. He has devoted his whole life to railway service and his contribution to the railway preservation movement has been an enormous one.

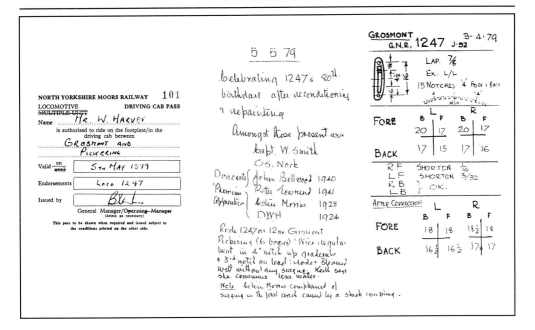

Bill Harvey's footplate pass on the NYMR, his diary entry recording the 20th Anniversary celebrations, and his characteristically thorough notes on his adjustments to 1247.

In addition to his Doncaster apprenticeship, his renown for precision and perfection owes much to the training and experience he acquired whilst working under L. P. Parker, the Locomotive Running Superintendent of the Eastern Region of BR. In his appointment as Shedmaster at Norwich from 1946, Bill became a legend through his devotion to, and affection for, the railways of East Anglia. That devotion was responsible for his refusal to accept promotion which would have required him to move away from Norwich.

When Thompson Class 'B1' locomotives Nos 1040-1052 were new, ex-Works, they were allocated to Norwich, and it can justly be claimed that in Bill's care they proved to be the finest on BR. At that time those locomotives were personally allocated to their own footplate crews which contributed greatly to their performance and the pride taken in their appearance.

Similarly in 1951, 'Britannias' Nos 70006-70013, 70034 and 70035 were allocated new, ex-Works, to Norwich where they gave exceptional service through the inspired care of Bill Harvey.

Life with 1247 was always full of pleasant surprises, and one day in 1979 I found a gentleman at Grosmont shed taking careful stock of the engine and making notes on his pad. It transpired that he was a Project Engineer/Designer with Hornby Hobbies, and he told me that they were proposing to produce a model of a Class 'J52' for their 00 range. In due course production commenced, and in July 1981 the model emerged bearing the number 1247. It was a good model and Hornby very kindly sent me one of the first off, together with another 'piece-small' to illustrate their methods of construction. The locomotive in GNR livery has now been discontinued, but they have recently introduced a version in lined black LNER livery with the number 3980 which is reminiscent of the appearance of 'the Old Lady' when I first made her acquaintance at Top Shed in 1959.

6.
A NATIONAL CELEBRITY

By 1980, traffic development on the NYMR called for seven- and occasionally eight-car trains to deal with peak season passengers, and therefore use of 1247 promised in future to be limited to low season and 'Santa Special' traffic. This caused me to review the future employment of the locomotive, particularly as neither of my sons showed an inclination to follow in my footsteps to a point where they would care for the locomotive in the event of my 'departure'!

Even one's demise is no excuse for allowing a historical relic to rust into oblivion, and I believed it only fair both to the brave little veteran and to posterity to ensure that 'the Old Lady' was placed in a secure and permanent resting place. This seemed to me to be the reasonable thing to do, since I had always considered myself to be merely the fortunate custodian, privileged to care for the locomotive and enjoy her company, rather than her proprietor. And so it was that I wrote to Dr Coiley at the National Railway Museum to ask if 1247 would be acceptable for his National Collection at York.

Dr Coiley's agreement to accept 1247 at the NRM caused no problems for the NYMR who by now had at their disposal more North East Locomotive Preservation Group-maintained engines, together with numerous individually owned locomotives. But it was in many respects sad to think that in future 'the Old Lady' could be providing a static, rather than a working, example of our steam heritage.

For transfer to York, 1247, with Driver John Bellwood and Fireman Kim Malyon, worked the last passenger train of the day from Grosmont, the 16.55 to Pickering. The engine remained for the night in New Bridge Yard before being loaded next morning on to a low-loader. The journey by road in 'light steam' was only as far as Dunnington, where the engine was re-railed on to the Derwent Valley Light Railway. Full steam was raised and 1247 was used to haul a Stephenson Crossley 0-6-0 diesel shunter acquired by the NRM from the Electricity Generating Board at Carrington Power Station to Layerthorpe. At that point, although still in steam, a BR diesel hauled the 'J52' and the shunter across the East Coast Main Line to the Railway Museum entrance, in compliance with BR requirements. But it can be said that 'the Old Lady' arrived at the NRM both in steam and in working order which, so far as I was concerned, was of paramount importance. A thorough 'NRM-type' clean transformed a working locomotive into an exhibit worthy of display in the world's finest railway museum.

My acquisition and care of 1247 over a period of 21 years, which came to an end in 1980, provided me with a strong body of good friends and an army of acquaintants.

In October 1980, 1247, with Driver John Bellwood, brushes her way along the overgrown Derwent Valley Light Railway *en route* to York and the National Railway Museum. (*National Railway Museum, York*)

'The Old Lady' is handed over to the Museum, December 1980. (Left to right) Dr John Coiley, Keeper of the Museum, myself, and John Bellwood, Chief Mechanical Engineer. (*by courtesy of The Yorkshire Evening Press*)

Myself and my former charge photographed in the Museum after the handing-over ceremony. (*National Railway Museum, York*)

Through the locomotive I had seen countless days of enjoyment with BR personnel and the staff and volunteers of private railways. It can truly be said that railway preservation is all about people. They are drawn from all walks of life, religions and political persuasions, and bring with them the widest possible cross-section of skills and talents. They are also possessed of singular patience and determination in tackling the daunting tasks of planning, building and improvising over many long, tiring and sometimes frustrating years before they succeed in opening their particular 'dream' railway.

Each year sees more of those dreams come true, and today our preserved railways constitute a vital and major constituent in the important tourist and leisure industries. From that modest start in 1959, the railway preservation movement flourishes today as never before, actively supported by many who were not even born when 1247 left Top Shed for Marshmoor.

The importance of people in railway preservation has already been stressed, and it applied equally in relation to this story of a small shunting engine which, with the help of people, achieved so many 'firsts' and, in the manner of Cinderella, was transformed from an untidy 'maid of all work' to a much photographed lady and TV personality.

Whilst I accept the danger of naming names, it would be wrong to record this story without re-emphasising the kindness, guidance and immeasurable support of Colin Morris, Peter Townend and Frank Knight. Without their help and encouragement, very little, if anything, could have been achieved.

Through my involvement with 1247, I had the pleasure of meeting and getting to know that warm-hearted, amusing and talented photographer, Bishop Eric Treacy. I first met him with his camera in Howarth yard whilst he was President of the Keighley & Worth Valley Railway, and every subsequent meeting was an enlightening experience. Whilst reflecting upon that splendid railway, mention must be made of the effort and hard work expended over

many years by those untiring volunteers, Ralph Povey (currently President), Hubert Foster, Tony Cox and Richard Greenwood. They were responsible for establishing the foundation and framework of the railway as we can see it today.

Similarly, that early emerging and ambitious Bluebell Railway with its exciting extension to link up again with BR at East Grinstead owes so much to the efforts of the effervescent and untiring Peter Manisty, and Bernard Holden, Superintendent of the Line.

My involvement with the NYMR over the past 15 years has provided an opportunity to form many valued friendships. From its very inception, that railway has been a runner carrying 'top weight' in the Preservation Handicap by virtue of the length of its track and its location away from sources of voluntary labour. It would not have survived for long or reached its present level of busy professionalism without the vision and loyal involvement of those of their members with varied talents and great patience. Viscount Downe, Railway President since its formation, has heavy business commitments, but is ever available and ready to give guidance and enthusiastic support. In the formative years, Richard Rowntree, a long-serving Chairman, and Derek Sawyer who, as Treasurer, always succeeded in providing, with a smile, 'something for everything, most of the time' from an ever inadequate funding, must take great credit for the splendid railway which has emerged.

When he retired from the Treasurership, the NYMR paid tribute to Derek's contribution: 'Calm and judicious, he tempered the enthusiasm of some of his colleagues with constant reminders of the limits of the possible and gained the confidence of all of them. Just as important, he imparted the same unstinted confidence to all the authorities with whom he dealt on behalf of the Railway.'

During his Chairmanship in 1976, Richard Rowntree provided two oval aluminium plates suitably engraved to acknowledge the long and continuous railway service which 'the Old Lady' had given – they are affixed, one each, to the two front wheel-splashers. I cannot mention the NYMR without also recording the name of Les Barwick, a volunteer who for very many years has spent all his leisure time (often accompanied only by his black labrador) maintaining and repairing the permanent way and renewing bridges to withstand the demands made upon them by the increasingly heavy traffic patterns. If preservation ever needs a job specification for the Volunteer, I suggest merely a picture of Les at work in some remote spot amid the North Yorkshire Moors – it would say it all! His recent award, the MBE, is a tribute not only to his personal efforts, but also to so many others who work untiringly to preserve our railway heritage.

In the earlier attempts to rescue and repair the permanent way on our newly acquired private railways, the work was heavy and daunting, being carried out the hard way. Relaying had to be carried out by hand, sleeper by sleeper. Even a short quarter-mile length involved weeks of back-breaking work, followed by a long period of consolidation by traffic, with all the irritation of speed restrictions.

Since the 'seventies our railways have grown up and gradual but costly mechanisation now permits re-laying by the use of track panels, placed in position by crane, with the formation then consolidated by modern tamping machinery. This eliminates the 'back-ache', renders the job more attractive to the volunteer and reduces the time that speed restrictions need to be imposed over the re-layed section.

Whilst 1247 was dependent upon the use of BR tracks from 1959 until 1962, it must be acknowledged that we could not have gone on to achieve 21 years of steaming until 'retirement' to the National Railway Museum in 1980 without the use of the tracks of privately preserved lines. It is for this reason that those railway friends simply have to be mentioned. They, and many others like them, are the men behind the tracks which make up our many splendid private railways of today.

So, after her many exploits in private ownership, 1247 became in 1980 the first steam locomotive to be presented to the National Collection in working order by a private individual. Housed at the National Railway Museum at York, the engine is listed among the 'exhibits of special interest'.

A National celebrity. In the old Main Hall at the National Railway Museum. (*Gwyneth Shipley*)

As one of the early Members of the Friends of the National Railway Museum, it was customary for me to attend each AGM in York. Each year Derek Sawyer, our Treasurer, and I met and shared lunch together before going to the meeting – we still enjoy this annual lunch 'fixture'.

In the spring of 1982 I noticed that both Derek and Richard Rowntree repeatedly enquired as to whether I would be at the AGM in June. In spite of my assurances, their gentle enquiries persisted, but such was my trust in two good friends of long standing that I failed to sense anything suspicious in those repeated enquiries.

It is difficult to describe the shock which was in store for me that afternoon in the Lecture Room at the NRM where I was comfortably seated beside Richard and Derek. Lord Downe was presiding and the following extract from the minutes of that meeting describes what happened:

'The last item on the formal agenda was the presentation of Honorary Life Membership (our first) to Capt W. G. Smith RNR; a moment in time which Lord Downe said was important to himself personally. "Capt Smith was the first person in Britain, perhaps in the world, to preserve a truly historic steam locomotive and eventually to make a major contribution to the Museum and to the fellowship of people who preserve and appreciate railways." The tangible memento of the occasion was the presentation of a suitably inscribed replica of an original 1875 membership certificate of the Amalgamated Society of Railway Servants. This was accompanied by a framed colour photograph of GNR No 1247 in its final resting place in the NRM. In reply Capt Smith said that he was surprised and overwhelmed by the honour, and then modestly reflected for our delight upon the many helpful officials who had conspired with many a rule-bending happy accident to bring about the preservation of this veteran H. A. Ivatt locomotive.'

I was quite shattered by the thought that what I had over the years tried to do quietly should have been observed by my friends to a degree where they felt disposed to extend to me so great an honour. Lord Downe is a master in the art of dealing with matters of that nature, and the manner of his doing so left me with a proud and memorable experience. The framed Certificate is treasured and hangs above the desk in my study.

Whilst I hope that many years of opportunity lie ahead, it will take my very best efforts over the remainder of my life to repay the Friends for the signal honour they showed me that afternoon. It is a comforting thought that when I can no longer do so, 'the Old Lady' will still be at York, ready and able to carry on the good work of supporting the Museum without me.

7.
THE 'PIONEER'

Throughout six years of glittering static display in the museum at York, the small shunting engine enjoyed its fair share of visitor attention among that superb collection of far more glamorous loco-motives. Whenever meetings took me to York over that period I contrived to arrive in sufficient time to pay 'the Old Lady' a short visit – such old friends are too valuable to neglect.

Then in 1986 the decision was taken by the NRM to entrust the Humberside Loco Preservation Group at Hull with the task of lifting the boiler, which was last undertaken at Doncaster works in 1958, 28 years previ-ously. At the same time the opportunity was taken to re-tube the boiler so that the engine would then be available with a valid boiler certificate, should she be required for 'live' display in the future.

Unfortunately, due to a work-load of higher priority at Dairycoates, 1247 failed to re-emerge until the spring of 1990 and, judging by the number of messages which found their way back to me from members of the public visiting the NRM, she was missed. At Grosmont shed, some of the good-natured humorists, with which that happy place abounds, regularly assured me that razor blades they were using were clearly embossed '1247' on one side and 'J52' on the other.

At the point at which the engine returned to York from Dairycoates, the Museum was embarking upon its preparations for the Great Railway Show. Replacement of the roof to the Main Hall necessitated transfer-ring all exhibits to the Peter Allen Building or to Swindon, and the 'J52' was pressed into service in the role of 'Museum Pilot'. A visit by a BBC Television Unit one afternoon found the work of removal in full swing and a short excerpt on a *Blue Peter* programme caught 1247 propelling her old Top Shed-mate No 4468 *Mallard* into position.

So far as the visiting public is concerned, the Great Railway Show provided an excit-ing re-emergence of 'the Old Lady'. Custom-arily housed in the Pavilion of 'Work Horses and Record Breakers', she emerged periodic-ally to take her rostered turn 'in steam', duties being shared with *Rocket* and *Iron Duke*.

On Saturday 23 June 1990, the ARPS and British Rail joined forces to celebrate 30 years of standard gauge preservation and the opening of the first private railway at Middleton, Leeds. The celebration involved running 'The Middleton Pioneer' from King's Cross to Appleby and return, the opportun-ity being provided for passengers to de-train at Leeds on the outward journey to visit the Middleton Railway at Hunslet.

The 'Pioneer' departed King's Cross at 07.30 hauled by an 'Electra' Class '90' locomotive. Driver Dave Rollins, the King's Cross Leeds-link driver in charge of the locomotive, was a fitting choice for the job, being readily recognised by passengers as a fellow steam enthusiast who relaxes regularly by spending 'busman's holidays' driving on the Bluebell Railway. Dave was also a driver in the party which travelled to care for No 4472 *Flying Scotsman* in Australia.

By kind permission of Dr Coiley, 1247 was released from the Great Railway Show and conveyed by road from York to Hunslet on Friday 22 June 1990. Dave Burrows, a crew member with *Rocket* in Vancouver for Expo '86, was the NRM representative with the engine. Steam was raised and the locomotive prepared to allow a run up the line 'light' that evening to ensure that no problems could arise the next day when the visitors arrived. It must be remembered that the 'J52' represented the largest engine ever used on that preserved line.

On Saturday 23 June, 1247 shared passenger workings with Sentinel WVBTG No 54 (BR 68153) and on Sunday 24 June with ex-NCB 0-6-0 *Primrose*. All went well and so far as the ex-London visitors were concerned the Middleton Railway provided the only steam element in their day's travel. It had not been so intended. 'Black Five' No

44871 *Sovereign* set out 'light' from Carnforth for Leeds to work the Leeds/Appleby leg of the tour, but had the misfortune to fail *en route*. The customarily inventive and resourceful Peter Manisty did his best to persuade BR to split the train and utilise 1247 to work six cars to Appleby. Whilst I had complete faith in the locomotive's ability, wherever would we have found the water? For their part BR failed to see the humour behind the suggestion and the limelight prepared for *Sovereign* fell across the capable shoulders of a Class '47' diesel.

The weekend at Middleton provided a welcome surprise in enabling me to renew acquaintance with an old friend in Hudswell Clarke 0-4-0ST No 1 *Mirvale* in whose company I was last in 1978 at Grosmont shed where she had been for some years stored in the head-shunt. At Hunslet in June 1990 the locomotive presented a beautiful picture, lovingly re-built and re-painted, a credit to all whose time, expertise and affection had renewed her useful life.

Sunday 24 June was an equally successful

On the Middleton Railway, Sunday 24 June 1990, with a brace of two-wheelers. (*Keith Sanders*)

On the previous day, 1247 is seen with the ten-wagon 'unfitted' goods train, heading for the gradient and the waiting army of photographers, who collected £125 from among their ranks to be donated to the Railway funds. (*Keith Sanders*)

day and the visitors, above the seasonal average in numbers, enjoyed the spectacle of 1247 working the passenger service with the four-wheeled Middleton stock. The guard in charge of the train was Dr Fred Youell whom I last met when, as Chairman of the Railway Preservation Society (the forerunner of the ARPS), I visited the Middleton Railway in May 1962. The opening of the railway in 1960 was due entirely to Fred's foresight, and it is true to say that its continued existence and development over the following 30 years owes much to his guidance, sustained hard work and enthusiasm.

I took the opportunity of visiting the small mechanical workshop adjacent to the station and learned that plans are in existence to double its size in the foreseeable future. Though small by some private railway standards, it is particularly well equipped to support locomotive maintenance and repair. When Middleton are able to re-plan the machinery layout in the larger area envisaged, an excellent workshop will emerge.

With the completion of the passenger service on Saturday evening, 1247 set back on to a ten-wagon 'unfitted' goods train which had been marshalled in the station yard in readiness. The goods was worked forward through the tunnel, thence on to the 1 in 27 gradient, alongside which a large gathering of photographers was waiting and jostling for position. Three runs were made for their benefit, by which time every camera had had its fill and the engine was 'disposed'.

It was with considerable surprise that I learned shortly afterwards that, arising from a collection among their number, the photographers had gathered the sum of £125 and donated it to Railway funds. A similar exercise on the evening of Sunday the 24th raised a further sum of £55. Never before had I heard of such gestures from that section of the steam train loving community of whom I had for so long been critical. It was a most generous and appreciated gesture. A glance at the bunker revealed that the coal

consumption to provide the photographic opportunities left little, if any, profit, but it was a splendid Middleton Railway/gricer' exercise and at the end of the day that was all that really mattered.

On the morning of Monday 25 June, 'the Old Lady' was re-loaded on to a low-loader for the short return journey by road to York and a resumption of duty in the Great Railway Show. All in all the weekend proved a first-class PR exercise for our National Railway Museum, seen in a supporting role to one of the smaller private railways. They don't have to be big to be beautiful!

I find it pleasing to occasionally ponder the thought of all that has happened since Works No 4492 was first laid down in Glasgow in 1899. All those whose skill and toil contributed towards her building will, no doubt, have passed on to that 'happy railway in the sky', but evidence of their skill is perpetuated in the continued exploits of 'the Old Lady'. Never could they have dreamed that the result of their labours would be there and still working for us to see in 1991.

Similarly, thought and credit must be given to H. A. Ivatt, whose knowledge and expertise almost 100 years ago was responsible for designing this large and highly successful class of 'workhorses' of which 1247 remains the sole survivor.

Finally, Dr Coiley's foresight in 1986 in authorising boiler repairs to the locomotive, coupled with the frustrating delay in execution of that work at Hull, may prove to be a great blessing. The consequent delay in provision of a ten-year boiler certificate until 1990 could mean that, in the absence of something unforeseen, 1247 should be capable of appearing in steam in 1999, her 100th year.

APPENDIX: 'J52' DRAWINGS AND DIMENSIONS

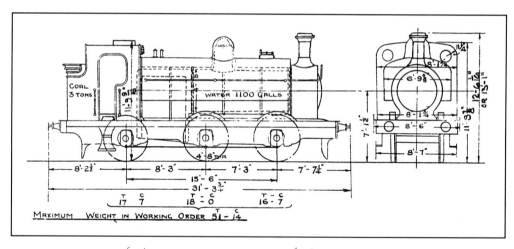

	ft	in		ft	in		
Grate			outside dia of smokebox	5	1¹/8	Springs — laminated	
length of slope	4	10	outside length of			3 ft 6 in centres	
width	3	4¹/4	smokebox	2	7³/4	9 plates, 4 in x ⁵/8 in	
grate area	16.25 sq ft		length between			Cylinders	
Firebox			tubeplates	10	9³/4	number	2
height of crown above			Small tubes (steel)			diameter	18 in
foundation ring			number	213		stroke	26 in
front	5	8¹¹/16	outside dia	1³/4 in		Motion type	Stephenson
back	5	2¹¹/16	thickness	11 WG		Type of valve	flat
interior length at top	4	8⁵/8	Heating surface (sq ft)			Max travel of valve	3¹³/16 in
interior width at boiler			firebox	103		Steam lap	⁷/8 in
centre	3	8	tubes	1,061		Exhaust lap	line & line
thickness of copper plates			total	1,164		Cut-off in full gear	75%
sides and back		⁹/16	Two 2¹/2 in dia Ross pop safety valves			Tractive effort (at 85%	
tubeplate		1⁹/16	Working pressure 170 lbs per sq in			of boiler pressure)	21,735 lbs
Boiler			Axles diameter length (in)			Total adhesive weight	115,808 lbs
outside length of firebox	5	6	journals 7¹/2 7			Total adhesive weight	
outside width of bottom	4	0¹/2	crank pins 7¹/2 4			————————— 5.33	
maximum dia of barrel	4	5	coupling pins			tractive effort	
length of barrel	10	6	leading 3 3¹/2			Brake — vacuum	
thickness of barrel plates		⁹/16	driving 3¹/2 4¹/4				
thickness of wrapper plates		⁹/16	trailing 3 3¹/2				

INDEX